LUDWIG VAN BEETHOVEN

**An Illustrated Biography
by
Ernst Herttrich**

VERLAG BEETHOVEN-HAUS BONN

Publications of the Beethoven House Bonn

Printed with gracious support of the
Landschaftsverband Rheinland

Selection of pictures with the kind assistance of
Silke Bettermann

English translation and bibliography by
J. Bradford Robinson

© 2000, Verlag Beethoven-Haus Bonn
Cover design: vice versa Cologne, Conny Koeppl
Production: Jütte-Messedruck Leipzig GmbH

ISBN 3-88188-060-7

CONTENTS

CHILDHOOD AND YOUTH IN BONN
1770–1792

Ludwig van Beethoven was born in Bonn in December 1770. The exact day is unknown. The only surviving document on his birth is an entry in the baptismal register of the Church of St Remigius in Bonn. This entry is dated Sunday, 17 December 1770, but the infant Ludwig may well have been born on the previous evening. Later in life, when asked about his birthdate, Beethoven was inconsistent in his answers. He also caused confusion by occasionally stating that he was born in 1772. The baptismal register is reproduced in plate 1 on page 7. Beethoven's parents are listed in the left column: *Joannes van Beethoven. & Helena* (actually Maria Magdalena) *Keverichs,* with the term *conjuges* added for "married couple." To the right are his godparents (Patrini): *Ludovicus van Beethoven* (the grandfather) *& Getrudis Müllers dicta Baums,* the wife of the Beethovens' next-door neighbour, Johann Baum.

Ludwig was his parents' second child. A first-born son, Ludwig Maria, was baptized about one and three-quarters of a year earlier, on 2 April 1769, but died after six days. Their third and fourth children were also sons: Kaspar Anton Karl (1774–1815) and Nikolaus Johann (1776–1848). Both eventually followed their brother to Vienna and played important if not always commendable roles in his life. After Nikolaus Johann, Beethoven's mother gave birth to three further children, two daughters and a son. All of them died in infancy.

At the time of Beethoven's birth, the family was living in the rear of a building then registered as Bonngasse 515. They did not remain there long, however, and frequently changed residence in the years that followed. One reason for this was surely the increasing size of the family. Another was probably the precarious financial straits in which they lived. Beethoven's great biographer, A.W. Thayer, felt that his father "might have lived in more comfortable circumstances had he seriously wished to do so. Besides his salary, however modest it may have been, he disposed of the inheritance from his father and the income from the lessons that must have fallen his way. His flighty and unstable nature bore the blame for the dire conditions into which he eventually descended."

Born in 1739 or 1740, Johann van Beethoven had been a singer in the Bonn court chapel from 1752. He was appointed a "court *musicus*" in 1756, and from 1764 he was a tenor with a fixed annual salary; he also played the violin and the piano. In 1767 he married the nineteen-year-old Maria Magdalena Keverich, a young widow from the town of Ehrenbreitstein opposite Koblenz.

Beethoven's family originated in Flanders and the Brabant, where the name is documented from the sixteenth century. Their family tree can be seen on page 8 (plate 2). Beethoven's grandfather, likewise named Ludwig (1711–1773), was the first to take up the musical profession. He was accepted as a choirboy at the koralen Huis of Mecheln Cathedral on 10 December 1717. Toward the end of 1731, he became a tenor in the choir of the principal town church in Louvain. Hardly a year later he moved to Liège to become a bass in the choir of St Lambert's. There he was heard by Clemens August, the Prince-Elector in Bonn, who as Archbishop of Cologne was also Bishop of Liège. Clemens August promptly retained Ludwig for his court chapel in Bonn. The young man began service in March 1733 and advanced to the position of court chapel-master in 1761. Besides his musical duties, he also ran a retail outlet for wine and was a respected citizen of the town. Beethoven had a high opinion of his grandfather and had his portrait sent to Vienna in 1801. The original, an oil painting by Leopold Radoux, is preserved today in the Vienna Historical Museum. A copy by Toni Blücher is reproduced on page 9 (plate 3).

Beethoven received his first musical training from his father. The lessons were probably not always pleasant for the boy. Gottfried Fischer, a master baker in whose parental home the Beethoven family lived from 1776, painted a vivid picture of them in his memoir of 1838: "Ludwig van Beethoven again began to receive daily lessons on the violin. One day he was playing by ear. His father came in and said: What sort of nonsense are you scratching? You know I can't stand it. Scratch the music on the page or your scratching won't do you much good."

Nonetheless, the boy made such rapid progress on the piano that his father had him appear in public in Cologne on 26 March 1776. The announcement of this concert is reproduced on page 10 (plate 4). A glance at it reveals that he reduced his son's age by some fifteen months, presumably to draw attention to a prodigy of Mozartean proportions. This was, in all probability, Ludwig's first appearance in public. It quickly became clear to his father that the boy's musical education should be entrusted to more competent teachers. Several names occur in this connection

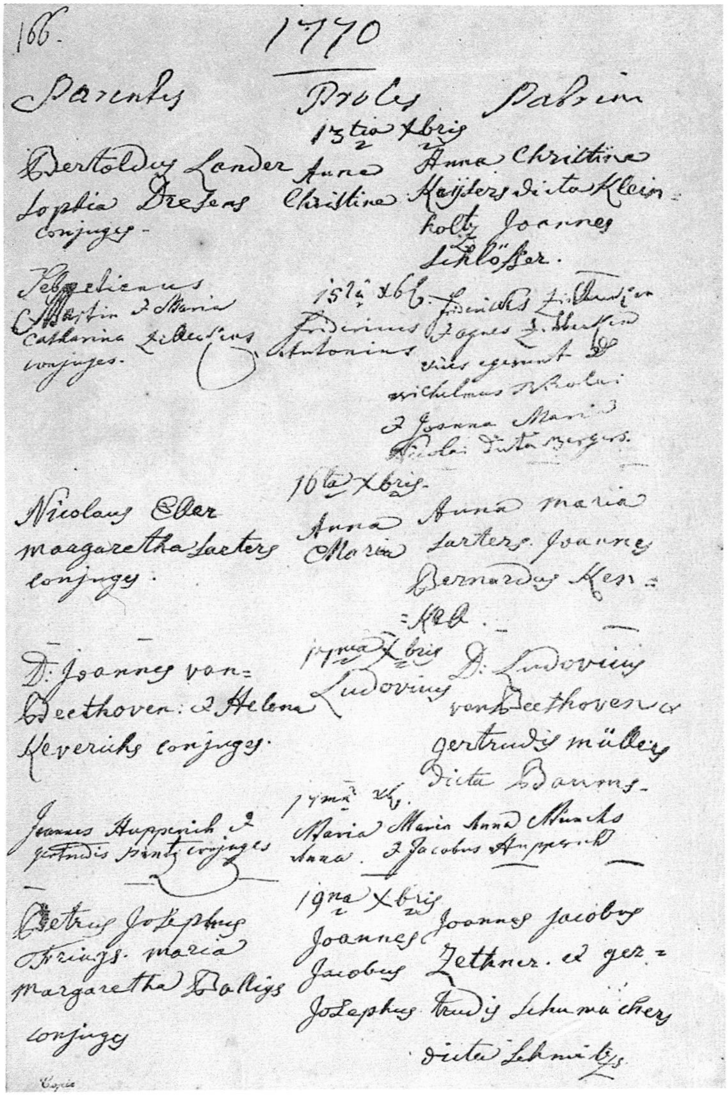

Plate 1
Page from the baptismal register
Bonn City Archive

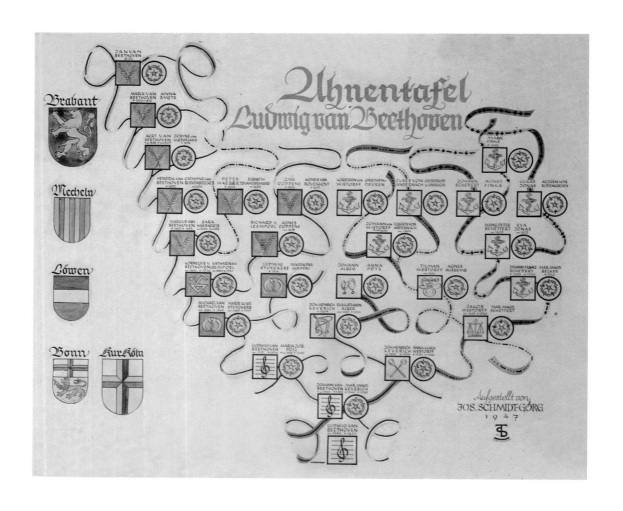

Plate 2
The Beethoven family tree
Beethoven House, Bonn

8

Plate 3
Beethoven' grandfather
Copy by Toni Blücher of an oil portrait by Leopold Radoux
Beethoven House, Bonn

Plate 4
Announcement of Beethoven's first appearance in public
Photo-reproduction of the original, destroyed by fire in 1960
Beethoven House, Bonn

in contemporary reports, not all of them equally substantiated. It is known that the court organist, van der Eeden, took charge of the boy's lessons from 1778. He was followed by Tobias Friedrich Pfeiffer, a tenor at the court theater and, to judge from contemporary accounts, "a polished pianist and an outstanding player of the oboe." The young violinist Franz Georg Rovantini gave the boy lessons on the violin and viola until his early death in 1781. Thereafter Beethoven took violin lessons from Franz Ries, a member of the court chapel. But it is generally agreed that Beethoven's most important teacher in Bonn was Christian Gottlob Neefe (see plate 5 on page 13). Writing in CRAMERS MAGAZIN DER MUSIK of 2 March 1783, Neefe spoke in glowing terms of "Louis van Beethoven ... a boy of eleven years and of most promising talent. He plays the pianoforte very skillfully and with power." Neefe claims to have "put Sebastian Bach's *Well-Tempered Clavier* into his hands" and given the boy "some lessons in figured bass." He was now instructing him in composition. To encourage his young pupil, Neefe had a set of "nine variations for pianoforte, written by him on a march, engraved at Mannheim. This youthful genius is deserving of help to enable him to travel. He would surely become a second Wolfgang Amadeus Mozart were he to continue as he has begun." The work in question is the *Variations pour le Clavecin sur une Marche de Mr Dresler*, published by Götz in Mannheim toward the end of 1782 (see plate 6 on page 14). In Beethoven's catalogue of works, this set of variations bears the number WoO 63 ("WoO" stands for "Werk ohne Opuszahl" = work without opus number). It was Beethoven's first work to appear in print. Writing some time between late 1792 and late 1793, the twenty-two-year-old composer thanked Neefe "for the advice you often gave me about making progress in my divine art. If I should ever become a great man, it shall partly be your doing" (letter no. 6 in the complete correspondence).

Neefe himself recorded that he allowed Beethoven to deputize for him as court organist from 1782. By 1784, when the boy was fourteen, he held a permanent position as court organist with an annual salary of 150 gulden. His first employer was Prince-Elector Max Friedrich, who ruled the electorate of Cologne-Bonn from 1761 to 1784. A portrait of the elector, by J. E. Marteleux, appears in plate 7 on page 15. Beethoven dedicated to him the three so-called "Kurfürstensonaten" WoO 47, published 1703 by Boßler in Speyer (see plate 8 on page 16). The successor of Max Friedrich, Maximilian Franz, was the youngest son of Empress Maria Theresia of Austria. It was he who introduced Viennese music (primarily Haydn and Mozart) to the Bonn court. He also enlarged the orchestra and theater and became the young Beethoven's most avid patron. An anonymous portrait of Maximilian Franz is reproduced on page 17 (plate 9)

Beethoven's duties in Bonn were many and varied. Not only did he play the organ at court and at the Minorite Church (along with Neefe), he was also a rehearsal pianist at the theater and played the viola in the orchestra. Fischer, the master baker whom we already had cause to mention, described his appearance years later as "short of stature, broad-shouldered, short-necked, with a large head, round nose, and dark-brown complexion. He always walked with a stoop." Fischer goes on to describe the young man's attire on duty: "a sea-green frock coat, knee breeches with buckles, stockings of white or black silk, shoes with black bowknots, a vest of embroidered white silk with pocket flaps, a short waistcoat, the vest decorated with a gold cord, hair curled and pigtailed, a crush hat under the left arm, and a sword on the left with a silver belt." Beethoven in rococo livery: that is not how we usually imagine him today. Instead, we tend to picture Beethoven as an unbridled revolutionary who freed himself from the feudal dress code. But it is useful to recall that this is the world in which he grew up. It helps us not only to understand his early compositions, but to appreciate his lifetime achievement. The inked silhouette on page 18, by Joseph Neesen, shows the sixteen-year-old composer with "short waistcoat ... his hair curled and pigtailed" (plate 10).

While carrying out his duties in Bonn Palace (see page 19, plate 11), Beethoven also tried to complete his general education, which until then had received short shrift. He established contacts with new circles. In the early 1780s he became acquainted with Franz Gerhard Wegeler, a young man five years his senior. Wegeler was important to Beethoven in several respects: he introduced him to the von Breuning family, and he became a faithful confidant even in his later years. Wegeler was also one of Beethoven's first biographers. The von Breunings were a respected Bonn family. The father had lost his life in a fire at Bonn Palace in 1777. Thereafter, Canon Johann Lorenz von Breuning became head of the family to prevent the widow, Helene von Breuning, from having to raise her four children alone. Two of these children, Eleonore (1772–1841) and Lorenz (1777–1798), became Beethoven's piano pupils. Eleonore later married F. G. Wegeler. Beethoven soon became a regular visitor at the hospitable and cultured home of the von Breunings, who gave him intellectual stimulation and an emotional haven from the troubled

C. G. NEEFE.

Plate 5
Christian Gottlob Neefe (1748–1798). Beethoven's teacher in Bonn
Engraving by Gustav Georg Endner (1778)
Beethoven House, Bonn

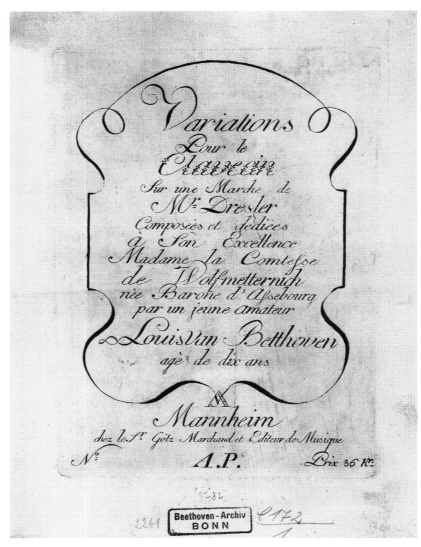

Plate 6
Ludwig van Beethoven, Variations for Piano, WoO 63
Title page of first edition
Beethoven House, Bonn

Plate 7
Maximilian Friedrich, Count of Königsegg-Aulenburg (1708–1784)
Archbishop and Prince-Elector of Cologne from 1761
Oil portrait by Joseph Engelbert Marteleux (c. 1780)
Beethoven House, Bonn, on permanent loan from Bonn City Museum

Plate 8
Ludwig van Beethoven, Kurfürst Sonatas, WoO 47
Dedicated to Elector Maximilian Friedrich. Title page of first edition
Beethoven House, Bonn

Plate 9
Maximilian Franz, Archduke of Austria (1756–1801)
Archbishop and Prince-Elector of Cologne from 1784. Anonymous oil portrait
Beethoven House, Bonn

Plate 10
Ludwig van Beethoven
Inked silhouette by Joseph Neesen, c. 1786

Plate 11
Residential Palace in Bonn. Tinted engraving
Beethoven House, Bonn

relations in his own family (see plate 12 with the portrait of Helene von Breuning and the medallions of her two sons Christoph and Stephan on p. 21).

This haven became all the more necessary after the death of Beethoven's mother. The young composer had set off for Vienna in 1787, probably in March, with the aim of taking lessons from Mozart. The great biographer Otto Jahn has handed down Mozart's comments when Beethoven first played for him: "Keep your eyes on him; some day he will give the world something to talk about." Admittedly there is no firm evidence that Beethoven ever took lessons from Mozart. Ries, in his biographical notes co-written with Wegeler, is somewhat vague on this point (page 86): "During his first stay in Vienna he received some instruction from Mozart." In any case, this instruction cannot have lasted long, for Beethoven was forced by his mother's illness to break off his visit in April. Returning by way of Augsburg, he met the local Baron von Schaden, to whom he confided his feelings on 15 September (letter no. 3): "I found my mother still alive, but in the most miserable state of health. She had tuberculosis, and died some seven weeks ago [on 17 July 1787] after enduring much suffering and pain. She was such a good, kind mother to me and the best of friends. Who was happier than I when I could still speak the sweet name of mother and it was heard and answered? To whom can I say it now?"

We know very little about Beethoven's life in Bonn after his return from Vienna, a period of no fewer than five and a half years. His circle of friends and acquaintances expanded. Besides many musicians from the court chapel, he also befriended the brothers Karl and Gerhard Kügelgen, both painters, and several members of the court retinue. Foremost among the latter was the young Count Ferdinand Ernst Gabriel Waldstein (1762–1823). Wegeler later described Waldstein and his relations with Beethoven (Wegeler-Ries, pp. 13f.): "He was not only a connoisseur but a practitioner of music. It was he who first truly appreciated Beethoven's gifts … From him Beethoven received much pecuniary assistance, bestowed in such a way as to spare his sensibilities, it being generally looked upon as a small gratuity from the Elector. Beethoven's dispatchment to Vienna by the Elector was actually the Count's doing. When Beethoven, at a later date, dedicated to him the great and important Sonata in C major, op. 53, it was only a proof of the gratitude which lived on unimpaired in the mature man.

At the end of 1792 Beethoven again set out from Bonn for Vienna. His friends compiled an album for him at his departure. In it, Waldstein wrote the following famous words (see plate 13 on page 23): "My dear Beethoven, you are about to trav-

20

Plate 12a
Helene von Breuning.
Oil portrait by Gerhard von
Kügelgen (ca. 1790)
Beethoven House, Bonn

Plates 12b and c
Medallions of Christoph and
Stephan von Breuning
Photographs after lost miniatures
from c. 1790
Beethoven House, Bonn

21

el to Vienna in fulfillment of your long frustrated wishes. The genius of Mozart is mourning and lamenting the death of her pupil. She found a refuge but no occupation in the inexhaustible Haydn; through him she wishes to form a union with another. With the help of assiduous labor you shall receive Mozart's spirit from Haydn's hands. Bonn, 29 October 792. Your true friend, Waldstein."

To a nature less robust than Beethoven's, these sentiments might have been a stifling and insurmountable burden. They had, however, a firm basis in reality. Haydn had visited Bonn in December 1790 while on his first journey to England. It is likely that Beethoven showed him one or both of his most lengthy compositions at that time: his cantatas on the death of Joseph II (WoO 87) and the ascent of Leopold I (WoO 88). The composition is said to have been "especially esteemed by Haydn, who encouraged its author to continue his studies" (Wegeler-Ries, pp. 15f.). The lessons with Haydn may have been arranged at that time. Whatever the case, these arrangements were certainly made no later than July 1792, when Haydn again stopped in Bonn on his return from London.

But this was far in the future. For the moment, Beethoven still had to fulfill his duties in the court chapel. He also had to help support his family. With the death of his mother, Beethoven's father increasingly lost hold on himself. Beethoven had no choice but to become, in a manner of speaking, the head of his family. In 1790, at his request, half of his father's annual salary was paid to him, along with three bushels of wheat belonging to this annual stipend. The fact that he was able to persevere in his creative work despite these adversities, and in addition to his many obligations at court, is an achievement that cannot be appreciated highly enough. The extent of his compositional output in Bonn was long underestimated. Besides the cantatas mentioned above, these included: a piano concerto of which only the soloist's part and a piano reduction of the orchestra have survived (WoO 4); a large-scale ballet jointly conceived with Count Waldstein and known as the *Ritterballet* ("Knights' Ballet," WoO 1. A facsimile of Beethoven's own piano reduction can be seen on p. 24, plate 14); many pieces for solo piano; and several items of chamber music, including three piano quartets (WoO 36) and two piano trios (WoO 37 and 38). He also wrote three concert arias (WoO 89, 90, and 92) and a great many lieder. Some of these compositions were published in Bonn by Simrock after Beethoven had left; many only appeared posthumously. Stylistically, they all betray the influence of the repertoire of the Bonn court chapel at that time. This repertoire was, however, surprisingly broad. The theater, although

Lieben Bethoven!

Sie reisen itzt nach Wien zur Erfüllung ihrer so lange
bestrittenen Wünsche. Mozart's Genius trauert noch
und beweinet den Tod seines Zöglinges. Bey dem uner-
schöpflichen Haydn fand er Zuflucht, aber keine Beschäf-
tigung; durch ihn wünscht er noch einmal mit jemanden
vereinigt zu werden. Durch ununterbrochenen Fleiß
erhalten Sie: Mozart's Geist aus Haydens Händen.

Bonn d 29t Octr. 792.   Ihr wahrer Freund Waldstein

23

Plate 14
Music to a Knight's Ballett, WoO 1, autograph piano reduction
No. 2 and 3: Deutscher Gesang and Jagdlied
Photo-reproduction of the original, destroyed by fire in 1960
Beethoven House, Bonn

dominated by Italians such as Paisiello, Piccinni, Sarti, and Salieri, also mounted operas and *opéras comiques* by French composers (d'Alayrac, Grétry, and Monsigny) and their German counterparts (Holzbauer, Schuster, and Umlauf). The instrumental repertoire consisted primarily of pieces from the so-called "Mannheim school" of Cannabich and Stamitz. However, pieces by C. P. E. Bach, Rosetti, Boccherini, Dittersdorf, and others were also heard. Beethoven's great exemplars were, of course, Haydn and Mozart. Their music increasingly found its way into the Bonn repertoire, especially during the reign of Maximilian Franz. It was on these two composers that Beethoven took his bearings, although he was still far removed from their mastery.

All the same, several of Beethoven's early Bonn compositions anticipate the style and expression of his later years. Among these are the Twenty-Four Variations on the Arietta "Venni Amore" by V. Righini, the Wind Octet in E-flat major (later published as op. 103), and in particular the Funeral Cantata on the Death of Joseph II. This latter work may be safely regarded as the culmination of Beethoven's Bonn period. When Brahms played through the piece after its rediscovery in 1884, he is said to have exclaimed, "Everything about it is Beethoven through and through; even if there were no name on the title page, no other composer would come to mind." Its fourth number, a soprano aria with chorus, is especially deeply felt. Later Beethoven incorporated its theme into the second finale of *Fidelio*. A number of works begun in Bonn were completed or revised in Vienna: the Second Piano Concerto, the String Trio op. 3, most of the lieder from op. 52, and perhaps even the Piano Trio op. 1, no. 1.

Early in November 1792 Beethoven left his home on the Rhine for Vienna to pursue his education. He could not have imagined that he would never see Bonn again. Elector Maximilian Franz had already proclaimed his willingness to maintain Beethoven's annual salary of 100 ducats. These payments continued until March 1794. In October, French troops marched into Bonn and the court was dissolved. When the area was reorganized politically at the end of the Napoleonic Wars, the former Cologne electorate was made part of the kingdom of Prussia. The resultant "Province of Rhenia" was governed from Koblenz.

In later life, Beethoven's letters to his Bonn companions could never quite suppress a sense of homesickness. For all his disorderly ways, he carefully preserved the mementos of his youth. Three and a half months before his death, in a letter of 7 December 1826 (letter no. 2236), he poured out his feelings to his boyhood friend Wegeler (see plate 15 on page 27): "Words cannot express the pleasure I felt in reading the letter from you and your Lorchen [Leonore von Breuning, his former piano pupil] ... I remember all the love you have always shown me – for instance, how you had my room whitewashed and thus gave me such a pleasant surprise – and likewise all the kindnesses I have received from the Breuning family ... I still possess Lorchen's silhouette, which should show you how precious to me even now are all the dear and beloved memories of my youth ... My beloved friend, this will have to do for today. Besides, I am overcome by memories of the past, and the letter you have just received is accompanied by a good many tears."

Plate 15
Franz Gerhard Wegeler (1765–1848). Drawing by Rudolf von Normann (1839)
Beethoven House, Bonn

THE FIRST VIENNA YEARS
1792–1802

Beethoven arrived in Vienna in early November 1792. At that time Vienna had some 220.000 inhabitants and was one of the largest cities in Europe. It was without peer as a musical capital, and its countless musical institutions exercised a magical attraction on composers and musicians, including vocal and instrumental virtuosos of all sorts. It needs hardly be added that the city had also spawned a mare's nest of contacts and intrigues, friendships and animosities, cliques and camps, in which the young Beethoven first had to grope his way.

Beethoven now had to do double duty as a student: besides becoming versed in the school of life, he still had to learn, or relearn, much of his art. He took lessons from Joseph Haydn, Johann Schenk, Johann Georg Albrechtsberger, and later even Antonio Salieri. This, too, is a notion we do not usually associate with Beethoven: this mighty creator of towering masterpieces now had to study with teachers who, Haydn apart, were far inferior to his artistic stature in every respect. In fact, like all men of genius, Beethoven spent his entire life learning his craft. He constantly studied the works of the great masters, above all Bach, Handel, and Mozart. Traces of these studies are legion in his music, especially in the late works. Even in the final weeks of his life he ordered a new edition of Handel's works to be sent from England.

Beethoven's lessons with Haydn (plate 16 on page 31) had, as mentioned above, already been arranged in Bonn. They began in early 1793 and probably lasted until shortly before Haydn's second departure for England on 19 January 1794. The notebooks in which he wrote his exercises still survive. They reveal that Haydn's primary concern was to teach his pupil the elementary rules of species counterpoint. They also reveal, however, that he applied these rules quite inconsistently, and at times must have caused more confusion than enlightenment in his pupil. The surviving exercises number well over 200. Of these, only about one-fifth have corrections in Haydn's hand. This leads us to conclude that the aging master was quite lax in his attitude toward these lessons and devoted little time to them. He was probably preoccupied with preparations for his next trip to England, especially in the latter half of 1793.

Beethoven must have been disappointed. Ferdinand Ries, the son of Beethoven's violin teacher F. A. Ries in Bonn and later his composition pupil, records the story that Haydn "wanted Beethoven to write 'Pupil of Haydn' on the title pages of his first works." Beethoven, he continued, refused, alleging that "although he had indeed received some instruction from Haydn, he had never actually learned anything from him." (Wegeler-Ries, p. 36) Elsewhere in his biography, Ries conveys the impression that relations between the two great composers were strained. This is rather unlikely. In August 1793, Haydn had his pupil accompany him to Eisenstadt, where he introduced him to Prince Esterházy, the man for whom Beethoven later wrote his great C-major Mass op. 86. Further, several entries in a small household chapbook that Beethoven kept in his early Vienna years reveal that the relations between the two men were thoroughly intact: "22 x. in chocolate for Haydn and me" he jotted down on 24 October. Finally, the op. 2 piano sonatas of 1796 – Beethoven's first work with opus number to be accepted by a publisher (the op. 1 piano trios had been engraved at his own risk) – do indeed bear a dedication to his former teacher. This said, it is no less true that in 1793, while he was still studying with Haydn, Beethoven secretly took lessons from Johann Schenk (1753–1836), a popular composer of light opera.

Beethoven's next teacher was Johann Georg Albrechtsberger (1736–1809; see plate 17 on page 32). Albrechtsberger taught the young man from January 1794 roughly until March 1795 in practically every area of counterpoint, using his own composition manual published in 1790. The surviving exercise books reveal the hand of a conscientious teacher.

Beethoven quickly gained entry into Vienna's musical circles. Some of the necessary contacts were probably made by his teachers, but he also came armed with recommendations from Bonn, especially from Count Waldstein. The recommendations opened many a door for him, particularly in aristocratic circles. But his musical abilities doubtless attracted attention as well. At first he was less valued for his compositions than for his prowess at the pianoforte. By this time, Beethoven was already a virtuoso of his chosen instrument. Thayer records the words of Abbé Joseph Gelinek, a famous pianist of the day who was bested in a contest with Beethoven: "Ah, he's not a man, he's a devil. He will play me and all of us to death. And how he improvises!" (Thayer, p. 139).

JOSEPH HAYDN.

Plate 16
Joseph Haydn (1732–1809), Beethoven's teacher from early 1793 to early 1794
Engraving by Carl Frederik Akrel (c. 1790)
Beethoven House, Bonn

Plate 17
Johann Georg Albrechtsberger (1736–1809)
Beethoven's teacher from early 1794 to early 1795
Engraving by Carl Traugott Riedel after a drawing by Lips (1803)
Beethoven House, Bonn

One of Beethoven's first patrons and friends in Vienna was Prince Karl von Lichnowsky (1761–1814; see plate 18 on page 35). Beethoven lived in the same house as Lichnowsky, first in an attic room and later in a ground-floor apartment; he was even a guest in the prince's own quarters from autumn 1794. Lichnowsky had been on close terms with Mozart; now Beethoven was to be his protégé. Beethoven expressed his gratitude by dedicating his op. 1 to the prince. Later, Lichnowsky also received the dedications of the piano sonatas op. 13 (the *Pathétique*) and op. 26, the variations WoO 69, and the Second Symphony. Writing to his boyhood friend Franz Gerhard Wegeler on 29 June 1801, Beethoven referred to Lichnowsky as his "warmest friend." He went on to mention that the prince had "granted me a guaranteed sum of 600 florins which I can draw on until I find a suitable appointment" (letter no. 65).

New acquaintances soon followed. One was Nikolaus Zmeskall von Domanovecz (1759–1833), an official at the Hungarian Court Chancery in Vienna and an accomplished amateur cellist. Zmeskall quickly gained the composer's affection. Beethoven wrote him many little notes and billets that reveal the warmth and good humor of his friendship – qualities not regarded as typical of Beethoven, but which are well-documented in his letters and many contemporary accounts. Another frequent butt of Beethoven's jibes and pranks, especially because of his corpulence, was the violinist Ignaz Schuppanzigh (1776–1830). His ample girth even inspired Beethoven to two little pieces of music: *Lob auf den Dicken* ("In Praise of the Fat Man," WoO 100) and the canon *Falstafferel, lass dich sehen* ("Wee Falstaff, come forth," WoO 184). The two young men – and they were still young in the mid-1790s – had met early in their careers, probably at the home of Prince Lichnowsky, where Schuppanzigh played first violin in the prince's quartet-in-residence. He remained among Beethoven's closest friends until the composer's death. As a concert organizer, Schuppanzigh was also one of the leading promoters of Beethoven's music, especially, as might be expected, of his string quartets (see plate 19 on page 36).

This is not the place to enumerate all the many friends and acquaintances Beethoven gained in his early Vienna years. A short list may suffice: Baron van Swieten, a friend of Mozart and the librettist of Haydn's *Creation* and *The Seasons;* Prince Lobkowitz, who would later play such a signal role in Beethoven's life; and the Stein-Streicher family of piano manufacturers. Beethoven was by no means the sullen loner that he is often made out to be. He was not only a much sought-after pianist, but a convivial man who quickly found his way into many social circles, both large and small.

Having used his first year in Vienna primarily to perfect his craftsmanship and cultivate a rich nexus of personal contacts, Beethoven devoted the next few years to writing new works of music. These years witnessed the birth of his three piano trios op. 1, his three piano sonatas op. 2, the first version of his Piano Concerto op. 19, a large number of dances for Vienna's carnival season, several lieder, pieces for woodwind instruments, arias for the theater, and other works. He seemed intent on trying his hand at every new genre and form. It is thus not surprising that he should take lessons, both now and later, from Antonio Salieri in the art of Italian vocal composition. The result was a large number of Italian songs for one or more voices, with or without accompaniment. Sadly, these works are hardly ever heard today.

Beethoven did not actually appear before the general public until 1795, when he played his B-flat major Piano Concerto in two concerts. The first was held on 29 March 1795 "for the benefit of the widows of the Musicians' Society;" the second was a "grand musical academy" given by Joseph Haydn on 18 December. A page from the B-flat major Concerto, in Beethoven's hand, appears on page 37 (plate 20). Another venture into the public eye was the publication of his three piano trios op. 1 in the summer of that same year. This was the first work that Beethoven considered worthy of bearing an opus number.

It was no coincidence that Beethoven's first appearance at a public concert had a charitable purpose. Beethoven had a lifelong fondness for such causes. One reason was perhaps the memories of his own childhood, when his father failed as a breadwinner and the boy was forced to provide for himself and his siblings. As it happened, his father died shortly after Beethoven had left Bonn. His sole surviving siblings, his brothers Kaspar Karl and Nikolaus Johann, likewise moved to Vienna in 1794 and December 1795, respectively. Here they expected assistance and support from their elder brother. The remnants of Beethoven's family were thus reunited. This was doubtless a source of comfort to the composer, for to a certain extent Beethoven always remained a "family man" who even late in life sought contact with families.

Plate 18
Prince Karl von Lichnowsky (1761–1814). Anonymous miniature
Beethoven House, Bonn

Plate 19
Ignaz Schuppanzigh (1776–1830). Unsigned caricature.
A simple flap allowed the thin figure to be transformed into a fat one
Gesellschaft der Musikfreunde, Vienna

Plate 20
Ludwig van Beethoven, Piano Concerto no. 2, op. 19. Autograph piano part
Beethoven House, Bonn, H.C. Bodmer Collection

Plate 21
The instruments of Beethoven's string quartet
given to him as a present by Prince Lichnowsky c. 1800
Beethoven House, Bonn
On permanent loan from the State Institute of Musical Research, Preussischer Kulturbesitz

The next few years were, for Beethoven, very busy and fruitful. In the first half of 1796 he travelled via Prague, Dresden, and Leipzig to Berlin. Among his many works of this period, both large and small, were the op. 5 Cello Sonatas, the Piano Sonatas opp. 7, 10, 13, and 14, the String Trios opp. 8 and 9, the op. 12 Violin Sonatas, the Piano Concerto op. 15, and the Wind Septet op. 20. The end point and culmination of this period were surely his First Symphony op. 21 and, most of all, the six string quartets op. 18. Both these opuses were published in 1801, the symphony by Hoffmeister and Kühnel's so-called "Bureau de Musique" in Leipzig, the quartets by Mollo in Vienna. These works are generally regarded as marking the end of his first important creative period and betoken his emancipation as an artist. It was at this time, probably to accompany the genesis of the string quartets, that Beethoven received a generous gift from Prince Lichnowsky: a complete set of valuable string quartet instruments, including two violins and a cello of Italian provenance and a viola probably built by J. A. Gedler of Füssen. A picture of them appears on page 38 (plate 21).

All in all, Beethoven's first ten years in Vienna were entirely successful. A miniature portrait on ivory by the Danish painter Christian Horneman (plate 22, page 41) shows Beethoven in the year 1802. Though thoughtful in his facial expression, he is immaculately clad and fashionably coiffured, a young-looking thirty-two-year-old gentleman at the height of his powers. Yet the end of this initial decade in Vienna was overshadowed by the first symptoms of his hearing impairment. Beethoven mentioned it in a letter of 1 July 1801 to his friend Carl Amenda, asking him to keep the matter secret (letter no. 67; see plate 23 on page 42):

"Your Beethoven is leading a very unhappy life and is at odds with Nature and his Creator. I have cursed Him many times for exposing His creatures to the merest chance, which is often enough to crush and destroy the loveliest blossom. Let me tell you that my most prized possession, *my hearing,* has greatly deteriorated. Even while you were still with me I could feel the symptoms, but I kept them to myself. Now they have become worse, and it remains to be seen whether my hearing can ever be restored … I hope it can, but the chances are slight. Such illnesses are the most difficult of all to cure. You can imagine what a sad life I am now leading. I have to avoid everything dear and precious to me and associate with such wretched egoists as Zmeskall, Schuppanzigh and their ilk … I have to withdraw from everything, and my best years will pass by without my bringing forth all the things my talent and strength have commanded from me. It is a sad realization in which I have had to seek my solace. Of course, I am resolved to rise above all of this, but how should I go about doing it? ... <u>I beg you to treat this matter of my hearing as a great secret and to disclose it to no one, no matter who it may be.</u>"

This moving document plainly illustrates two basic traits of Beethoven's character: his proneness, perhaps conditioned by his hearing ailment, to outbursts of misanthropy and distrust that did not even spare his closest friends (Zmeskall and Schuppanzigh surely did not deserve his castigation), and his unyielding will to persevere and master his fate in the teeth of adversity. The famous "Heiligenstadt Testament," written at the beginning of October 1802 in the Viennese suburb of Heiligenstadt (whence it takes its name), lends expression to these same feelings. It also reveals that Beethoven correctly assessed, and suffered from, the bad impression he often left on his fellow beings (letter no. 106):

Oh ye who regard or proclaim me to be malevolent, obdurate, or misanthropic,
you do me a grave injustice ...

Though born with a fiery and boisterous temperament, even susceptible to the diversions of society, I was soon compelled to keep myself apart and to conduct my life in solitude. If ever I tried to surmount these woes, oh how cruelly I was flung back by the doubly unhappy realization that I am hard of hearing. It was not yet within my powers to say to people, "Speak more loudly, shout, for I am deaf." ...

Imagine my humiliation when someone standing beside me
heard a flute in the distance and I heard – nothing! ...

Such incidents brought me to the verge of despair,
and there was little to prevent me from putting an end to my life.
The only thing that stayed my hand was my art.
Ah, I found the thought intolerable that I should leave the world
before I had brought forth all I felt capable of achieving.
So I endured this wretched existence ...

Divine One, thou lookest down upon my inmost being; thou knowest that therein dwells a love of mankind and a desire to do good. And you, my fellow men, when you come to read this one day, consider that you have dealt me an injustice. May the poor unfortunate take comfort in finding one of his own kind who, despite all the obstacles of Nature, nevertheless did everything within his powers to be admitted into the ranks of worthy artists and men...

Plate 22
Ludwig van Beethoven. Miniature of 1802 by Christian Horneman
Beethoven House, Bonn, H. C. Bodmer Collection

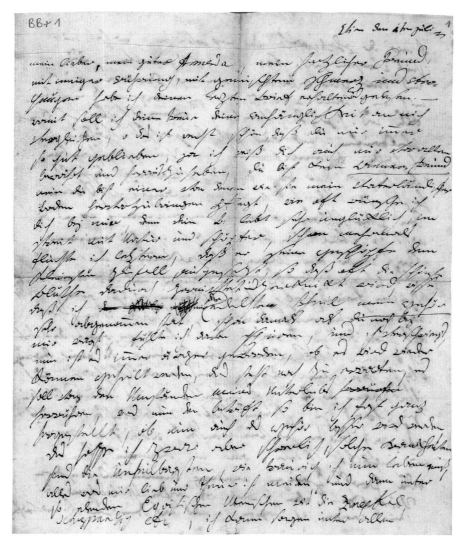

Plate 23
Beethoven's letter of 1 July 1801 to his friend Carl Amenda
Beethoven mentions the onset of his deafness
Beethoven House, Bonn, H.C. Bodmer Collection

"There is only one Beethoven"
1802–1812

That Beethoven was able to compose at all, despite his deafness, has always been a source of amazement. However, as he wrote to Amenda, his ailment "hindered him least of all in the act of composition." What is deserving of admiration is not only his ability to compose – this was a matter of technique – but above all the mental achievement of wanting to compose at all. Beethoven's creative powers were undiminished. He was, to use an outdated expression, in the prime of life. It is no coincidence that Willibrord Joseph Mähler, in his great oil portrait of 1804, depicts the composer with right hand outstretched, seemingly grasping life by the throat (see plate 24 on page 45). Perhaps this is one reason why Beethoven took such a liking to the painting and kept it on display in his lodgings to the end of his days. "Dear Mähler," he wrote the artist that same year (letter no. 206): "I most earnestly request you to return my portrait to me as soon as you have made full use of it [perhaps to have it copied?]. Should you still need it, please at least make haste: I have promised it to a lady from abroad who saw it here and wants to have it in her room during her stay of several weeks in Vienna – and who can resist such <u>charming advances?</u> It is clearly understood, of course, that some of the <u>favors this will bestow on me</u> will fall <u>your</u> way. Wholly your Beethoven."

Beethoven and women! It is almost a journalistic commonplace to chide artists for their libertine relations with the opposite sex, and to excuse them with a knowing wink. With Beethoven, this is not quite the case. The topic of "Beethoven and Women" usually never gets far beyond his famous letter to the mysterious "Immortal Beloved." The notion of Beethoven in love, paying court on bended knee, does not fit our received image of the composer. Yet this notion is thoroughly in accord with reality. In the spring of 1799, Beethoven made the acquaintance of the von Brunsviks, a family from the Hungarian aristocracy. The middle daughter, Josephine, became his piano pupil. Countess Josephine was briefly married to Joseph Deym, likewise an Hungarian aristocrat, who died in the early part of 1804. By late summer Beethoven was quite obviously paying court to the young widow, who at first did not turn a deaf ear to his advances. At the turn of the year 1804–5 he composed two lieder for her: "An die Hoffnung" ("To Hope"), op. 32, and "Andenken"/"Ich denke dein" ("Memento"/"I think of thee"), WoO 136. He then wrote a set of variations on the second lied, dedicating them to Josephine and her elder sister Therese. Portraits of the two sisters appear on pages 46 and 47 (plates 25 and 26). In the end, Beethoven's courtship foundered on the differences in their social station, for the Countess would have lost custody of her four children by marrying a bourgeois.

Josephine then entered an unhappy second marriage with an Estonian baron, Christoph von Stackelberg. On 12 July 1817 Therese confided to her diary: "Perhaps Josephine is being punished for Luigi's [i.e. Beethoven's] sufferings. His wife! Just imagine what she could have made of this towering hero!" Indeed, at the height of his relations with the beautiful countess, Beethoven himself regarded her as a sort of Muse. "For a long period," he wrote to her early in 1805 (letter no. 216), "a certain event made me despair of ever achieving happiness in this life on earth. Now things are no longer half as bad, for I have won your heart. I am fully aware of the value I must attach to it. I shall redouble my activities, and I promise you by all that is dear and sacred that I shall soon stand before you more worthy of myself and of you."

This "event" was, of course, the aforementioned onset of his deafness. Although Beethoven promised, in this letter, to "redouble his activities," he had by no means been inactive in the years since the Heiligenstadt Testament. In quick succession he had produced some of his best-known and most popular works: the Symphonies nos. 2 and 3 (the "Eroica"), the Third Piano Concerto, the two violin romances, the Triple Concerto, the piano sonatas opp. 31, 53 ("Waldstein"), and 54, the piano variations opp. 34 and 35, the violin sonatas opp. 30 and 47 ("Kreutzer"), and his oratorio "Christus am Ölberge." Further, he was about to embark on his first opera "Leonore," the early version of "Fidelio."

The opera cost him enormous toil, however, and its première performance was a fiasco. It took place at the *Theater an der Wien* on 20 November 1805 (see plate 27 on page 48) under the worst imaginable circumstances. Though famous as a composer of instrumental music, Beethoven was unknown as an opera composer. There were countless arguments with the singers, who considered their parts unflattering to the voice – an accusation which, in all fairness, is occasionally still heard today. Beethoven adamantly refused to make changes. Worse, the singers were still not, or no longer, at the forefront of their profession. Anna Milder-Hauptmann would later become a great artist and achieve special fame in the role

Plate 24
Ludwig van Beethoven. Oil portrait of 1804 by Willibrord Joseph Mähler
Vienna Historical Museum

Plate 25
Josephine, Countess Deym, née von Brunsvik (1779–1821)
Oil portrait by Johann Baptist Lampi the Elder ?

46

Plate 26
Countess Therese von Brunsvik (1775–1861)
Self-portrait after a painting by Johann Baptist Lampi the Elder, 1810
Beethoven House, Bonn

Theater an der Wien.   Théâtre sur la Vienne.

N.º 23.

Wien bey T. Mollo.

Plate 27
Theater an der Wien. Tinted engraving
Beethoven House, Bonn

of Leonore. At 20, however, her acting abilities left much to be desired. Contemporary critics agreed that the tenor, Demmer, was unequal to the role of Florestan, still less the bass Sebastian Mayer to that of Pizarro. Moreover, the circumstances in Vienna were hardly conducive to make the theater public eager to hear a new opera. On 13 November, exactly one week before the première, French troops had entered the city. The Vienna correspondent of Kotzebue's magazine DER FREIMÜTHIGE captured the feelings of its inhabitants:

> The entrance of the French in Vienna was, for the Viennese, an occurrence to which they could not at all become accustomed, and for several weeks a quite untypical silence reigned over the city. The court, its administrative offices, and most of the large landowners had moved elsewhere …
>
> The people could hardly be expected to give much thought to diversions, now that concern for survival was so all-powerful and the fear of confrontations and unpleasant incidents kept men and women alike in their homes. The theaters, too, were at first quite empty; gradually the French began to attend the performances, and even now they still make up the bulk of spectators.

The performance itself was reported in the LEIPZIGER ALLGEMEINE MUSIKALISCHE ZEITUNG, perhaps the leading German music periodical of its day: "The strangest item among last's months new musical products was doubtless Beethoven's long-awaited opera, *Fidelio oder Die eheliche Liebe.* It was, however, very coolly received … As Beethoven has sacrificed beauty at the altar of the new and strange on many earlier occasions, people were prepared above all to find novelty, idiosyncrasy, and a certain brilliant creative originality from this, the first of his vocal products for the stage. Yet precisely these qualities were least conspicuous … The vocal numbers are generally devoid of underlying new ideas; they are, for the most part, too long, the text is repeated *ad infinitum,* and they have a noticeable lack of characterization … The choruses are ineffective, and one of them, the chorus of prisoners on their enjoyment of a brief moment of freedom, is obviously botched. Nor was the performance distinctive. Dem[oiselle] Milder, despite the beauty of her voice, had far too little passion and vitality for the role of Fidelio, and Demmer's intonation was almost invariably flat. These factors taken together, and perhaps the current circumstances as well, ensured that the opera was heard only thrice."

These criticisms were seconded by several of Beethoven's friends after the fiasco of the première. Eventually the composer took them to heart – but fortunately not all of them, or even the "Prisoners' Chorus" so belittled by the critic of the Leipziger Allgemeine Musikalische Zeitung would have been scuttled. How tastes change! Beethoven set about reworking the piece, which was duly revived on 29 March 1806. The libretto was rewritten by Stephan von Breuning, Beethoven's boyhood friend from Bonn and a resident of Vienna since 1800. Breuning shortened the original three acts into two and rearranged several of the numbers. A few items of the first version vanished altogether. As so often happens in operatic history, the revised version found favor with the public, and it was repeated on 10 April – only to be withdrawn by the composer. Once again, his violent temper had proved his own worst enemy, and he angrily demanded the return of his score after an altercation with the theater director, Baron von Braun.

In the summer and autumn of that same year Beethoven, anxious perhaps to leave the occupied capital, made several journeys, not all of which are well documented. In the autumn he stayed at Prince Lichnowsky's country estate Grätz near Troppau in Silesia. Lichnowsky was still among the composer's staunchest supporters. In that very year, 1806, he had commissioned a large portrait of Beethoven from the Viennese painter Isidor Neugass (see plate 28 on page 51). Ironically, Beethoven was confronted by French occupying forces anyway: Lichnowsky's estate was commandeered by French officers, and the prince forced Beethoven to play for the assembled foreign guests. Even at the best of times Beethoven disliked such requests and seldom gave in to them. In this case he refused outright. An exchange of words ensued, and Beethoven left Grätz in the dead of night. Marching by foot, he arrived in Troppau in little over an hour and hurried back to Vienna by the next available post-coach. He is said to have left behind a note for the prince with the famous and much-interpreted words: "Prince, what you are, by accident of birth, I am by dint of my own efforts; there have been and always will be princes by the thousands, but there is only one Beethoven" (letter no. 258). However revolutionary and rebellious these words may sound, their intent was not political. Beethoven was primarily concerned to assert his own identity, not to question the *raison d'être* of the nobility. He felt quite at home among aristocrats and gladly availed himself of their services. At times he behaved far worse toward his own servants than any baron, count, or prince toward his subjects.

Having finished his labors on "Leonore," Beethoven again had time for other projects. The years from 1806 to 1808 witnessed the birth of one new work after another from his pen: the Piano Sonata op. 57 (the "Appassionata"), the 32 Variations

Plate 28
Ludwig van Beethoven. Oil portrait by Isidor Neugass, 1806
Beethoven House, Bonn
On permanent loan from the Ars Longa Foundation, Amsterdam

(WoO 80), the Cello-Sonata op. 69, Symphonies nos. 4 to 6 (see plate 29 on page 53), the "Coriolanus" Overture, the Violin Concerto, the Fourth Piano Concerto (see plate 30 on page 54), the Choral Fantasy op. 80, the "Rasumovsky" String Quartets op. 59, the C-major Mass op. 86, and a good many lesser pieces. On 22 December 1808 the *Theater an der Wien* mounted an "academy," i.e. a concert organized by Beethoven for his own benefit, in which he presented most of his new orchestral music. There were no fewer than eight items on the program, including three large-scale multi-movement works:

Before the intermission	*After the intermission*
1) Symphony no. 6, op. 68	5) Symphony no. 5, op. 67
2) Aria, "Ah! perfido," op. 65	6) Sanctus from the Mass in C, op. 86
3) Gloria from the Mass in C, op. 86	7) Improvisation for solo piano
4) Piano Concerto no. 4, op. 58	8) Choral Fantasy op. 80

It was a memorable event that placed severe demands on players and audience alike. The concert began at 6:30 and lasted until after 11 o'clock. The theater was icy cold, and the listeners sat in their boxes wrapped in coats and furs. The program was under-rehearsed. Beethoven had, to put it simply, attempted too much at once, and he did both himself and his art a disservice. The two symphonies and the concerto, in particular, had broken new ground in the handling of the orchestra, the writing for the piano, and the fabric of the music. These works burst the bounds of existing musical forms and pushed forward into uncharted territory, particularly in their expression. Of this, the audience at the première could only have had a faint inkling.

Before the concert took place Beethoven had completely fallen out with the singers and orchestral musicians. In these years he was considered uncontrolled and frequently ill-tempered; this, of course, was not conducive to winning new friends. He was also unhappy with his professional status, having still not found a permanent position at the age of 37. He often railed at his fate. It is therefore not surprising that when he was offered the position of court music director in Kassel, he was not at first disinclined to accept.

Plate 29
Ludwig van Beethoven, Symphony no. 6, op. 68. Autograph score
Beethoven House, Bonn

Plate 30
Ludwig van Beethoven, Fourth Piano Concerto op. 58
Title page of first edition
Beethoven House, Bonn

The Peace of Tilsit in July 1807 had given birth to a new Kingdom of Westphalia, and Napoleon, on 1 December 1807, proclaimed his brother Jérôme to be its first king. Jérôme was an avid music lover and much intent on ostentatious display. He founded an opera in his capital city of Kassel and offered the position of general music director to Beethoven in autumn 1808. Normally Beethoven would surely have dismissed such an offer in outrage; Kassel, after all, was woefully provincial compared to the musical metropolis of Vienna. But 1808 had not been a good year for Beethoven in Vienna, and for the moment he was tempted to accept. "I have received a fine offer to become court conductor to the <u>King of Westphalia,</u>" he wrote to his friend Baron Ignaz von Gleichenstein on 1 November 1808. "I am to be paid handsomely, and am asked to state how <u>many ducats</u> I want to receive" (letter no. 339). As late as 9 January 1809 Beethoven could inform his publisher Härtel (letter no. 350): "The intrigues, cabals, and all manner of infamies have at last forced me to leave what remains of my German fatherland. I have accepted an offer from His Royal Majesty of Westphalia to settle there as court conductor at a yearly salary of 600 gold ducats. This very day I have sent my assurance that I will accept, and am only awaiting my certificate of appointment before I make preparations for my journey, which will take me through <u>Leipzig.</u>" Whether Beethoven was telling the whole truth remains a moot point. No such letter of acceptance has survived, and by January the efforts of his friends to keep him in Vienna were well underway. In a contractual agreement of 1 March 1809 the composer was guaranteed an annual pension of 1800 florins from Prince Kinsky (plate 31 on page 57), 1500 from Archduke Rudolph (plate 32 on page 58), and 700 from Prince Lobkowitz (plate 33 on page 59) – a total of 4000 gulden. In return, he promised to remain in Vienna.

The purpose of this agreement was to grant Beethoven the financial independence he needed to devote himself entirely to his profession and to "create only large and sublime works ennobling to his art." In the event, however, it was to prove a source of worry and annoyance. The Napoleonic Wars and the French occupation of Austria made it necessary for the country to reform its currency in early 1811. Austria's money was reduced to a fifth of its former value. Beethoven immediately set about trying to recover his loss of income. At first, a new arrangement was drawn up that seemed decidedly in his favor. Before long, however, even greater difficulties arose. Prince Kinsky died on 2 November 1812 from the complications of a riding accident, and Prince Lobkowitz's financial situation deteriorated drastically, due partly to the currency reform and partly to his own mismanagement.

Not until the spring of 1815 did Beethoven again receive regular payments from the Kinsky family and Prince Lobkowitz.

This "pension," of course, was not Beethoven's only source of income. By June 1801 he could already proudly report to his boyhood friend F.G. Wegeler: "It is safe to say that I almost have more commissions than I can possibly carry out. What is more, I can reckon with some six or seven publishers for each of my things, or even more if I want. People no longer negotiate with me; I state my price and they pay" (letter no. 65). True to form, Beethoven was exaggerating: he often had to tone down his requested fees enormously. But he was much in demand for his compositions and had no difficulty in finding publishers for them. In his early Vienna years he generally entrusted them to local publishing houses; now he sought contact with publishers abroad. Between 1809 and 1812, for example, almost all his works were issued by the famous house of Breitkopf & Härtel in Leipzig (see plate 34 on page 60 for a portrait of Gottfried Christoph Härtel). Among these works were most of the pieces heard at his "academy" of December 1808 (apart from opp. 58 and 65), along with the Fifth Piano Concerto, the vocal score of "Leonore," the Third "Leonore" Overture, the incidental music to "Egmont," the oratorio "Christus am Ölberge," the String Quartets opp. 74 and 95, the Piano Sonatas opp. 78, 79, and 81a ("Les Adieux"), and a number of lieder.

One of Beethoven's most famous compositions from this period, his piano piece "Für Elise," was never published during his lifetime. There is a theory that he wrote this little bagatelle for Therese Malfatti, and that the original title on the presentation manuscript (unfortunately no longer extant) read "Für Therese." This theory has never been proved, and new studies reveal that the piece may have originated at another time. But even if false, the theory is not far-fetched: Beethoven was in close contact with the Malfatti family in 1809–10, having probably been introduced to them by his friend Baron Ignaz von Gleichenstein. Johann B. Malfatti had been Beethoven's physician from early 1808. Beethoven gave lessons to his younger daughter Therese and indeed left her the manuscripts of some unpublished pieces. He even went so far as to propose to the young lady, probably in the middle of May. Therese declined: she apparently did not reciprocate his feelings. Nor was he the right match for this affluent family, which had been elevated to the nobility in 1804. A portrait of Therese Malfatti appears on page 61 (plate 35). Her rejection plunged Beethoven, as he wrote to Gleichenstein (letter no. 445), "from the heights of sublime ecstasy to the depths of despondency ... It is therefore only in my own

Plate 31
Ferdinand Johann Nepomuk Kinsky, Prince of Wchinitz and Tettau (1781–1812)
Lithograph by Joseph Kriehuber (1828)
Beethoven-House, Bonn

Plate 32
Archduke Rudolph of Austria (1788–1831), Cardinal and Archbishop of Olmütz
Oil portrait after Johann Baptist Lampi the Elder, c. 1820
Beethoven House, Bonn

Plate 33
Franz Joseph Maximilian, Prince Lobkowitz (1772–1816)
Oil portrait by F.A. Oelenhainz
Roudnice castle

Plate 34
Gottfried Christoph Härtel (1763–1827)
Photograph after a lost oil portrait by Ferdinand Georg Waldmüller
Beethoven-House, Bonn

Plate 35
Therese Malfatti (1792–1851)
Photograph of an anonymous pastel portrait
owned by the von Gleichenstein family
Beethoven House, Bonn

heart that I can again find sustenance and support; there is none to be had from the outside ... Well, so be it! For you, poor Beethoven, there is to be no happiness from without. You must create everything you want in yourself; only in the Ideal World will you find friends."

It has been assumed that the passionate String Quartet in F minor, op. 95, was written under the impress of Beethoven's disappointment. This assumption may well be justified. The first sketches arose in the early part of summer 1810. Even the remarkable subtitle, "Quartetto serioso," lends weight to this supposition. So does Beethoven's remark, in a letter to the English conductor George Smart, that the quartet was written only for a small circle of connoisseurs and should never be played in public.

Beethoven was slow to recover from his despondency. Astonishingly, he then produced some of the most beautiful, vibrant, and cheerful works in his entire œuvre: the Piano Trio op. 97, the Seventh and Eighth Symphonies, and the Violin Sonata op. 96. But the next crisis was already at his doorstep. Again, it was a love story, and again it had a negative outcome. In summer 1812 Beethoven visited the spas of Bohemia – Teplitz, Karlsbad, and Franzensbad – in the hope of restoring his health. He had arranged a meeting with the Brentano family in Karlsbad. On 6–7 July, writing from Teplitz, his first stopping point, he penned his famous letter to the "Immortal Beloved" (letter no. 582):

My angel, my all, my self. –
Only a few words today …

Why this profound sorrow when necessity speaks?–
The only way our love can endure is through sacrifice,
by renouncing our desires.
Can you alter the fact that you are not wholly mine, and I am not wholly yours? –
Dear God, look at Nature in all her beauty and calm your heart at what must be –
Love demands all, and rightly so.
Thus it is for me with you, and for you with me. –

Ah, there are moments when I find that words are as nought –
Be cheerful, and be my ever-faithful, my only sweetheart, my all, as I am yours.
The gods must send us everything else, the fate that must and shall be ours …

Good morning, on July the 7th –
Even while still in bed my thoughts rush to you, my Immortal Beloved,
now joyful, now sad, waiting to know whether Fate will hear our prayer. –
I can only live entirely with you or not at all.
Yes, I have resolved to wander aimlessly abroad until I can fly to your arms
and feel at home in their embrace, until you can lift my soul to the Spirit Realm,
enfolded in your midst –
But alas, it must be. You shall soon be calm, the more so as you know my loyalty to-
ward you. No other woman can ever possess my heart …

What tearful longing for you – you – you – my life - my all. –
Farewell, never cease to love me,
and never misjudge the most faithful heart of your beloved
Ludwig
ever yours   ever mine   ever ours

The identity of the "Immortal Beloved" has eluded scholars for generations. Even today, the mystery still remains unsolved. To all appearances she was a married woman, and Beethoven's letter is an act of renunciation obviously carried out with a heavy heart. Roughly at this time Beethoven began to maintain a diary. In it we can read, in words much like those we find in his letter to Gleichenstein after his rejection by Theresa Malfatti, "You must not be a human being, *not for yourself, but only for others:* for you there is no longer any happiness except within yourself, in your art." Beethoven's posthumous effects contained two anonymous miniatures that have frequently been linked to the unknown woman. These portraits are reproduced on page 65 (plates 36a and 36b). The first may depict Giulietta Guicciardi(36 a), the dedicatee of the "Moonlight Sonata," who was once occasionally thought to be the Immortal Beloved. The other (36 b) is more difficult to identify. Depending on the author's point of view, it is said to represent Josephine Deym, Antonie Brentano, or Countess Almerie Esterházy. Of the many names that have cropped up in the endless chain of speculations, only these two remain today. Josephine Deym, as mentioned above, had already received ardent love-letters from Beethoven in the winter of 1804–5, and by 1812 her second marriage had entered a serious crisis. Antonie Brentano was the wife of Bettine Brentano's stepbrother, Franz Brentano (see plates 37 and 38 on pages 66 and 67). Beethoven had come into contact with the family two years previously. Since then, their relations had become very close. Even in later years, long after the family had returned to Frankfurt, Franz Brentano occasionally gave Beethoven financial support. Antonie received several presentation copies of his works, including the autograph manuscript of the lied "An die Geliebte" ("To the Beloved One," WoO 140). This manuscript is still extant today; in her hand, it bears the words, "The 2nd of March 1812, Requested by me from the author." Beethoven later dedicated to her one of his mightiest creations, the Diabelli Variations op. 120. Further, it was Franz and Antonie Brentano who, in 1820, commissioned what is probably the most famous of all Beethoven portraits from the Munich court painter, Joseph Karl Stieler (see plate 47 on page 85). Oddly, the portrait never entered the possessions of the Brentano family. – The third woman, Almerie Comtesse Esterházy, has only recently been brought into play (Oldřich Pulkert and Hans-Werner Küthen: Ludwig van Beethoven im Herzen Europas, Prague 2000). One searches in vain for her name in previous writings on Beethoven.

Plates 36a and b
Two miniatures, from Beethoven's estate
Beethoven House, Bonn, H.C. Bodmer Collection

Plate 37
Antonie Brentano (1780–1869)
Oil portrait by Joseph Karl Stieler (1808)
Brentano House, Winkel / Rheingau

Plate 38
Franz Brentano (1765–1844)
Oil portrait by Joseph Karl Stieler (1808)
Brentano House, Winkel / Rheingau

THE DEAF COMPOSER
1812–1824

It is tempting but dangerous to look for parallels between an artist's life and his art. Such relations are extraordinarily varied and complex. Artists differ enormously in this respect: Goethe wrote his "Karlsbad Elegies" to extricate himself from a severe depression, while Mozart, at a time of extreme material need, wrote the vibrant "Jupiter" Symphony and his comic opera "Così fan tutte." Beethoven compensated for Therese Malfatti's rejection of his suit by writing the "Quartetto serioso" in F minor, only to follow it with such exuberant works as the Seventh Symphony and the Archduke Trio. Now he had to free himself from the crisis wrought by his self-imposed renunciation of the Immortal Beloved.

For a long time nothing seemed to work, and the years immediately following July 1812 were conspicuously barren. Hardly any major new pieces arose at this time. Instead, Beethoven busied himself with revising works which were, for the most part, already complete: the two symphonies, the Piano Trio, and the Violin Sonata. He neglected his appearance. Nannette Streicher, a Viennese piano manufacturer on close terms with the composer, is said to have found him "in the summer of 1813 in the most desolate state as regards his physical and domestic needs … Frau Streicher, after her return to the city, put his wardrobe and household affairs to rights and, with the help of her husband, saw to the provision of the necessities … Beethoven obeyed in every particular." (Thayer, p. 554) Nor were his business affairs successful: he was forced to borrow money from Franz Brentano, and his plans to hold academies in April or May came to nought. Maynard Solomon, in his biography of 1977, was surely right to maintain that "by mid-1813, Beethoven had fallen into a state of mental and physical disorder that drastically affected his musical productivity." (p. 285)

Then, on 27 July 1813, the news reached Vienna of an event that would fundamentally alter both Beethoven's life and the history of the Napoleonic Wars. The combined forces of England, Spain, and Portugal, under the leadership of General Wellington, dealt Napoleon his first serious defeat near the town of Vittoria in northern Spain. This news was doubly important for Beethoven as he had a special relation to Napoleon. Originally he was an ardent admirer of Napoleon the statesman and planned make him the dedicatee of the "Eroica" Symphony. But no sooner had he learned of Napoleon's proclamation as Emperor in May 1804 than he allegedly tore the title page of the finished manuscript in two and threw it to the ground. According to Ries's biography (Wegeler-Ries, p. 78), Beethoven cried out: "Is he too nothing but an ordinary human being? Now he, too, will trample on the rights of man and indulge only his ambition. He will exalt himself above everyone else and become a tyrant!" The title page of the "Eroica," with the deleted inscription to Napoleon, is shown on page 71 (plate 39).

Napoleon's wars of conquest only confirmed Beethoven's altered opinion, and his defeat was occasion enough to celebrate the event in a large-scale musical "battle painting." The result was "Wellington's Victory, or the Battle of Vittoria," op. 91, and its première duly took place in Vienna on 8 and 12 December 1813. The success was overwhelming. This was not the only time in music history that a composer achieved popularity with works that posterity has found fit to disdain. Beethoven relished the cheers of the public. He confided to his diary that "it is certain that one writes more beautiful music as soon as one writes for the public, even when one writes quickly." It is a strange remark. By "beautiful" he surely meant "ingratiating" or "popular." Normally Beethoven considered his art sacrosanct and made no concessions to public taste. This diary entry gives some indication of just how great his "disorder" must have been.

Beethoven was now riding the crest of a wave of success. The Seventh Symphony was no less rousingly applauded than "Wellington's Victory." The premières of both works were quickly followed by many repeat performances. On 27 February 1814 the Eighth Symphony was premièred, and on 23 May the second and final revision of "Fidelio" went on the boards at the *Kärntnertor Theater,* likewise to the cheers of the audience. The Congress of Vienna opened on 18 September 1814, bringing further success and laurels to Beethoven from the assembled crowned heads of Europe (see plate 40 on page 72). Virtually all of them attended the "grand musical academy" he held on 29 November 1814. The program included not only the Seventh Symphony and the inevitable "Wellington's Victory," but the première of a large-scale cantata entitled "Der glorreiche Augenblick" ("The Glorious Moment"), the title page of which is reproduced on page 73 (plate 41). The cantata celebrated not only the peace for which the people had yearned for so many years, but also the assembled monarchs in the audience. Many Beethoven scholars view "Wellington's Victory," "Der glorreiche Augenblick," and other lesser works of this

Plate 39
Ludwig van Beethoven, Symphony no. 3, op. 55 ("Eroica")
Title page of engraver's copy
Archive of the Gesellschaft der Musikfreunde, Vienna

Der große Wiener Friedens-Congres zur Wiederherstellung von Freiheit und Recht in Europa

Scene from the Congress of Vienna. Tinted engraving
Vienna Historical Museum

72

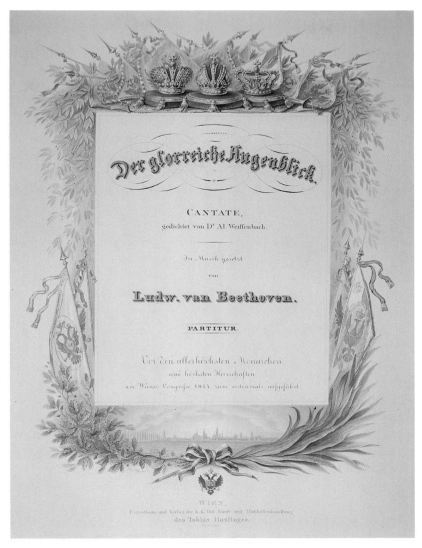

Plate 41
Ludwig van Beethoven, "Der glorreiche Augenblick," cantata, op. 136
Title page of first edition
Beethoven House, Bonn

period as what Maynard Solomon has called the "nadir of Beethoven's artistic career." *(Beethoven*, p. 287)

Now, these works can be judged from various angles. But Beethoven may well have been conscious of leaving what he so frequently called the hallowed path to true art in order to pursue popularity. Indeed, it may have been just this awareness that plunged him into another artistic crisis shortly after the *annus mirabilis* of 1814. Once the Congress of Vienna had come to a close on 9 June 1815, his major works of the next two years strike out on fresh paths and, to a certain extent, form a transition to his late style. They are almost exclusively pieces of chamber music: the two Cello Sonatas op. 102, the Piano Sonata op. 101, and the song cycle "An die ferne Geliebte," op. 98. Other works include a few isolated songs and canons and "Meeresstille und glückliche Fahrt," a setting of two Goethe poems for chorus and orchestra. Revealingly, perhaps, several large projects of this period – a new symphony, a sixth piano concerto, and a new opera – were never completed.

We have somewhat lost sight of Beethoven's two brothers. The younger, Nikolaus Johann, had trained to be an apothecary in Bonn and completed his pharmaceutical studies in Vienna. In 1808 he purchased an apothecary's shop in Linz. He turned a handsome profit during the Napoleonic Wars as a provisioner to the army, and was able to buy a large country estate in Gneixendorf near Krems in 1819. The older brother, Kaspar Anton Karl, became a civil servant after attempting, without success, to follow in his brother's footsteps as a musician and composer. He was frequently helpful to Beethoven in his negotiations with publishers and occasionally prepared piano reductions of his scores. In 1806 he married Johanna Reiss. Johanna's reputation was not untarnished, and Beethoven mistrusted her from the very start. The couple's only child was born in that same year. Then Kaspar Karl died on 15 November 1815. His will appointed Beethoven to serve as guardian of his nine-year-old son, Karl. In a codicil, however, he specifically stated that "it is not my wish that my son Karl shall be separated from his mother." A custody dispute soon arose between Beethoven and his sister-in-law. Though temporarily settled in Beethoven's favor on 19 January 1816, the case dragged on until well into 1820. The court's decision of January 1816 empowered Beethoven to separate the boy from his mother. Being unable to raise the boy in his bachelor quarters, he enrolled him in a boarding school under the tutelage of Cajetan Giannattasio del Rio. The next few years were marked by endless bickering over and with his young nephew. The boy, as was only natural, constantly sought contact with his mother; his uncle tried to prevent this at all costs. The quality of Beethoven's life during these protracted conflicts took a decided turn for the worse.

Meanwhile, his hearing continued to deteriorate. At a concert held on 25 January 1815, he accompanied the singer Franz Wild in a performance of his famous and popular song "Adelaide" at the request of the Czarina of Russia. It was probably his last public appearance as a pianist. The loss of his ability to perform music can only have had a severe effect on his mental state. It is frequently said that his creative powers suffered as well from all his adversities. As far as the years 1816 and 1817 are concerned, this was certainly the case. Apart from the aforementioned Piano Sonata in A major op. 101, very few works originated at this time: several lieder, canons, folk-song arrangements for an English amateur named Thomson (at least they were well-paid), variations for piano and flute for the same patron, and similar items. Only gradually did Beethoven's creative spirits return. Probably at the end of 1817 he started work on the great "Hammerklavier" Sonata in B-flat major, op. 106. Its first two movements were finished in the spring of 1818. As occasionally in earlier years, he then spent the summer months in Mödling near Vienna.

Nature outings were always very important to Beethoven. Charles Neate, a young musician from England who spent much time in Beethoven's company in the summer and autumn of 1815, later spoke of their walks through the countryside. Never, he told Thayer, had he "met a man who so enjoyed nature; he took intense delight in flowers, in the clouds, in everything. Nature was like food to him, he seemed really to live in it" (Thayer, p. 620). Once again, nature seems to have had a soothing effect on Beethoven, although by now he had become so deaf that most visitors could only converse with him in writing. August Karl Friedrich Kloeber (1793–1864), who painted a portrait of Beethoven during that same summer in Mödling (see plate 42 on page 77), later recalled his impressions in a short article for the ALLGEMEINE MUSIKALISCHE ZEITUNG (1864, no. 18, col. 324): "He was already quite deaf, and when I wished to say anything to him I either had to write it down or speak into his tube, unless his famulus, a young relative some twelve years of age [obviously Beethoven's nephew Karl], was present and could shout the words into his ear."

The "tube" was, of course, one of the ear-trumpets Beethoven had been using since late 1813 (see plate 43 on page 78). Written communications took place with the aid of small notebooks known today as the "conversation books." It was here that Beethoven's visitors wrote down their questions and replies (see plate 44 on page 79). Beethoven used these notebooks roughly from February 1818. Today, they are an inexhaustible wellspring of information for Beethoven scholars, even if the composer's part in these conversations was seldom put down in writing.

But advancing deafness did not prevent Beethoven from persevering in his art. He continued to work on the "Hammerklavier" Sonata, which he finally completed in the spring of 1819. The title page of the first edition appears on page 80 (plate 45). Then, in the same year, he probably embarked on the Diabelli Variations, op. 120. The initial plans for the Ninth Symphony probably originated at this time, too. They were, however, put aside for a new large-scale project, the "Missa solemnis," op. 123. On 4 June 1819 Archduke Rudolph of Austria, Beethoven's great patron and benefactor (he was also his piano and composition pupil), had been invested as Archbishop of Olmütz. Beethoven resolved to compose a grand Mass for the coronation ceremonies to be held on 20 March 1820. "The day," he wrote the Archbishop in his letter of congratulation, "on which a High Mass composed by me shall be performed during the ceremonies for Your Imperial Highness will be the most glorious of my life; and God will enlighten me so that my meager talents may contribute to the ennoblement of that solemn day." (letter no. 1292)

Plate 42
Ludwig van Beethoven, Pencil drawing by
August von Kloeber, 1818
Beethoven House, Bonn, H.C. Bodmer Collection

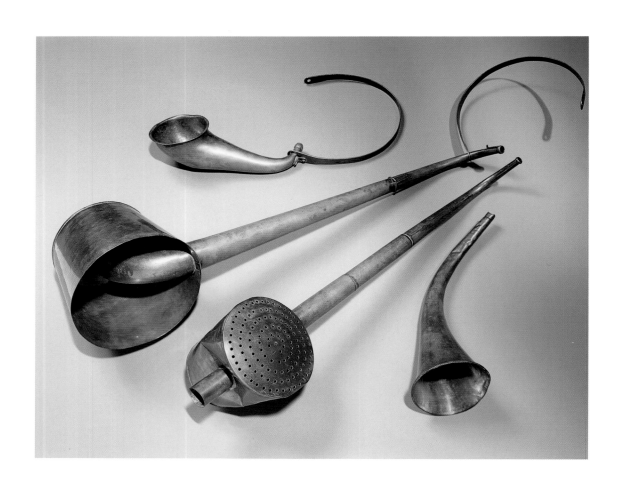

Plate 43
Beethoven's ear trumpets, manufactured at his request in 1813 by the inventor
Johann Nepomuk Mälzel
Beethoven House, Bonn

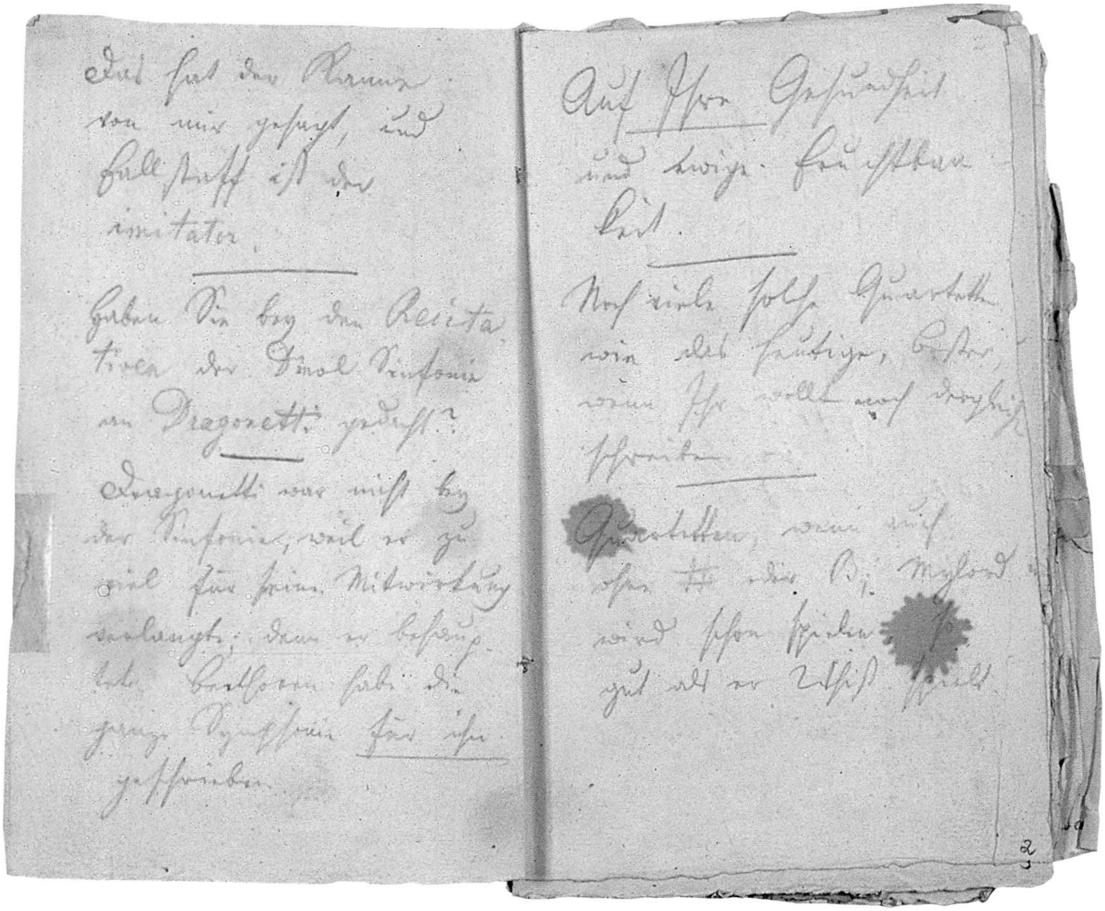

Plate 44
Page from Beethoven's conversation book no. 95 of 9 September 1825
Beethoven House, Bonn, H.C. Bodmer Collection

79

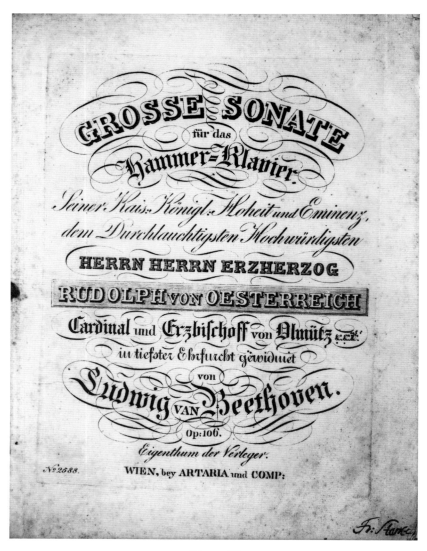

Plate 45
Ludwig van Beethoven, Piano Sonata in B-flat major, op. 106 ("Hammerklavier")
Title page of first edition
Beethoven House, Bonn

But the "Missa solemnis" was not to be completed until 1822. New disputes in connection with his nephew distracted him from his work. Most of all, however, the Mass assumed almost hybrid proportions far beyond anything he had produced to date. In the end, it burst the bounds of liturgical church music altogether. The surviving sketches alone occupy no fewer than ten large notebooks and an untold number of loose leaves. Hardly another composer left behind so many sketches as Beethoven; whether jotting down short ideas and inspirations or working out lengthy passages before committing them to paper, sketches formed an essential part of his creative process. One leaf from a "Missa solemnis" sketchbook is reproduced on page 84 (plate 46). Not surprisingly, he was unable to hand a copy of the Mass to its dedicatee until 19 March 1823. The first performance was given in St. Petersburg on 18 April 1824. Fittingly, the event took place, not in a church, but in a concert hall. The work did not appear in print until late 1826, when it was published by Schott in Mainz.

Beethoven invested enormous efforts in the "Missa solemnis." The importance he attached to this gigantic work is clearly in evidence in Joseph Karl Stieler's portrait, which shows the score of the Mass clutched in his hand (see plate 47 on page 85). Painted in February and March 1820, this is probably the most famous of all Beethoven portraits. It was presumably at Beethoven's insistence that he was shown holding the "Missa solemnis," which he surely regarded as his magnum opus to date. Stieler's handwriting has been identified on many pages of conversation books 7 to 10. The first of his entries opens with a request: "Please be so kind as to seat yourself as if you were writing in order to try out the position." Later we read: "It will take up too much of your time. What we've done today alone is enough for another sitting." We can well imagine that Beethoven was not a very patient subject at those sittings.

The three years that witnessed the gradual emergence of the "Missa solemnis" also brought forth several by-products: the Bagatelles op. 119, incidental music for "The Consecration of the House," a number of minor pieces, and above all the three late piano sonatas opp. 109 to 111. As in the "Hammerklavier," these three sonatas go far beyond the piano music of their day both in their expression and their demands on the player. A few years later, in January 1826, the piano builder Conrad Graf placed at Beethoven's disposal a grand piano with four strings per pitch because the conventional instruments no longer met his standards (see plate 48 on page 86). Besides the "Missa solemnis," Beethoven devoted the year 1822 primarily to the "Diabelli Variations." This great work may be said to represent his compositional legacy to the art of variation, and as such it stands alongside Bach's "Goldberg Variations."

In the event, Beethoven's major effort of 1823 was to be the Ninth Symphony. Like the "Missa solemnis," this mighty work broke the bounds of anything previously imagined in the symphonic genre – and not only because of its large-scale choral finale. Beethoven had toyed with the idea of setting Schiller's "Ode to Joy" while still in Bonn. Later we find initial thoughts on its setting jotted down at various places and times in his sketchbooks. The opening of the "Joy" melody, as sung by the solo bass, can be seen on page 87 (plate 49).

Anton Schindler, in his biography of 1845, reports that Beethoven originally wanted the Ninth Symphony to be premièred in Berlin. The reason, Schindler claims, had to do with various minor grievances and his annoyance at the Rossini craze that was sweeping Vienna at that time. When his plans became known in Vienna, thirty artists and art-lovers sent the composer a sort of letter of supplication in February 1824. In it, we can read: "Do not withhold the performance of your latest masterworks any longer from popular enjoyment, from those hungering for grandeur and perfection. We know that your great sacred composition has been followed by another ... We know that a new flower gleams in the garland of your glorious and still unequalled symphonies ... Do not allow these latest offspring of your genius to appear some day as foreigners on the native soil!"

Beethoven could hardly ignore these pleas. He acquiesced, and preparations were soon underway for an "academy." The Ninth was given its première performance at the *Kärntnertor Theater* on 7 May 1824. Besides the new symphony, the audience also heard the Overture to "The Consecration of the House," op. 124, and the Kyrie, Credo, and Agnus Dei from the "Missa solemnis," the latter three for the first time in Vienna. A playbill from this performance is reproduced on page 88 (plate 50). As it happened, the performance was flawed. The critic of the ALLGEMEINE MUSIKALISCHE ZEITUNG in Leipzig wrote: "But where shall I find the words to report on these gigantic creations to my gentle readers, particularly as the rendition was ... anything but satisfactory. Three rehearsals can hardly suffice for difficulties of this order of magnitude, and we have no cause to speak of impressive overall strength, proper distribution of light and shade, perfect command of intonation, subtle hues, or nuanced delivery. Even so, our impression was one of indescribable grandeur and nobility, and the audience heaped cries of ecstatic and unbridled jubilation upon the sublime master whose inexhaustible genius has opened up a new world to our eyes and unveiled to the sacred precincts of art wondrous secrets never before heard or divined!"

Contemporary observers record that Beethoven was on stage for the entire performance and exercised a sort of pro forma overall command. With his back turned to the audience, he was not even aware of the general excitement. Not until the alto soloist, Caroline Unger, grasped him by the arm and turned him toward the audience did he take a bow – and was thereupon uproariously applauded by everyone present.

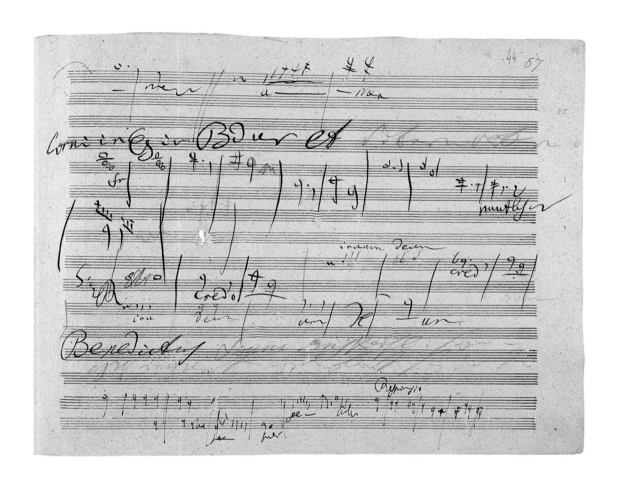

Plate 46
Ludwig van Beethoven, sketches for the "Missa solemnis."
The annotation alongside "Benedictus" translates as "may also be cheerful."
The Latin text has an underlaid German translation ("Gesegnet gelobet sej der")
Beethoven House, Bonn, H. C. Bodmer Collection

Plate 47
Ludwig van Beethoven. Oil portrait by Joseph Karl Stieler, 1820
Beethoven House, Bonn

Plate 48
Beethoven's last piano. Hammerklavier built by Conrad Graf in Vienna, 1825
Beethoven House, Bonn

Plate 49
Ludwig van Beethoven, Symphony no. 9, op. 125. Autograph score
Staatsbibliothek zu Berlin · Preussischer Kulturbesitz

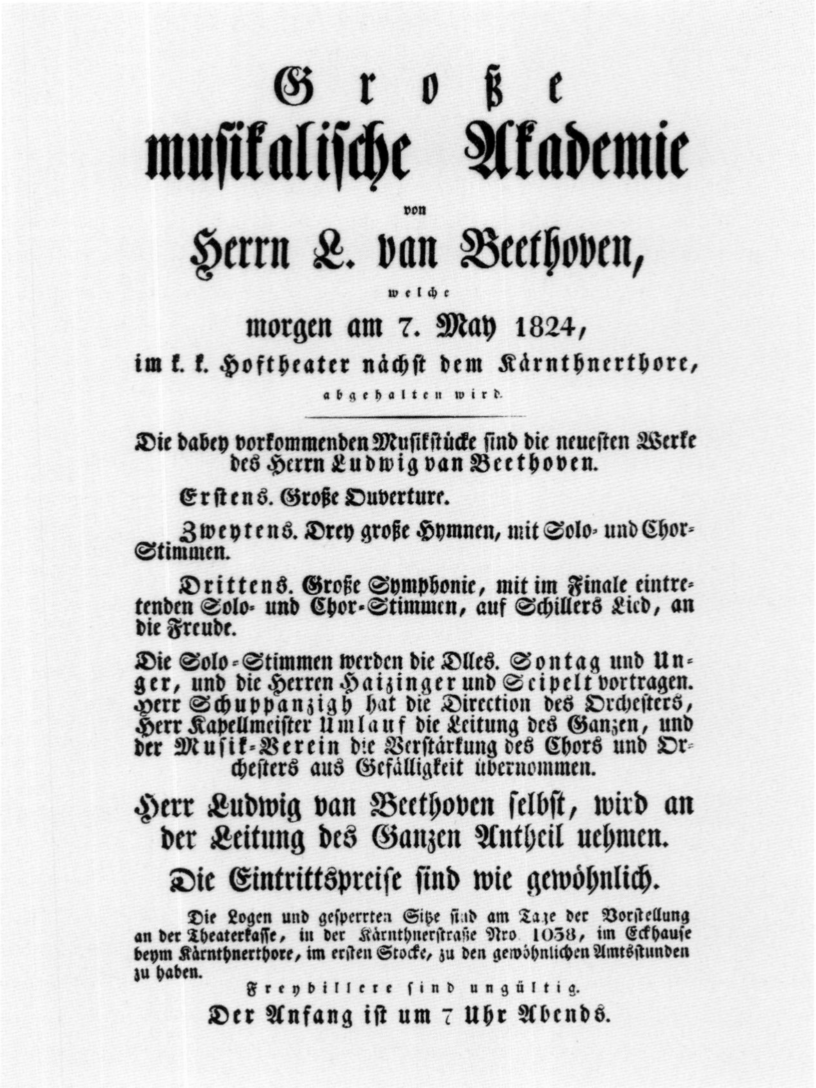

Große
musikalische Akademie

von

Herrn L. van Beethoven,

welche

morgen am 7. May 1824,

im k. k. Hoftheater nächst dem Kärnthnerthore,

abgehalten wird.

Die dabey vorkommenden Musikstücke sind die neuesten Werke des Herrn Ludwig van Beethoven.

Erstens. Große Ouverture.

Zweytens. Drey große Hymnen, mit Solo- und Chor-Stimmen.

Drittens. Große Symphonie, mit im Finale eintretenden Solo- und Chor-Stimmen, auf Schillers Lied, an die Freude.

Die Solo-Stimmen werden die Dlles. Sontag und Unger, und die Herren Haizinger und Seipelt vortragen. Herr Schuppanzigh hat die Direction des Orchesters, Herr Kapellmeister Umlauf die Leitung des Ganzen, und der Musik-Verein die Verstärkung des Chors und Orchesters aus Gefälligkeit übernommen.

Herr Ludwig van Beethoven selbst, wird an der Leitung des Ganzen Antheil nehmen.

Die Eintrittspreise sind wie gewöhnlich.

Die Logen und gesperrten Sitze sind am Taze der Vorstellung an der Theaterkasse, in der Kärnthnerstraße Nro 1038, im Eckhause beym Kärnthnerthore, im ersten Stocke, zu den gewöhnlichen Amtsstunden zu haben.

Freybillere sind ungültig.

Der Anfang ist um 7 Uhr Abends.

Plate 50
Playbill for the première of Beethoven's Ninth Symphony
Beethoven House, Bonn

ILLNESS AND DEATH
1824–1827

The première of the Ninth Symphony left Beethoven exhausted. The composition of this gigantic work, the preparations for its performance, the negotiations with the theater director, and the supervision of the copyists who wrote out the instrumental parts: none of this had left him unscathed. Worse, the problems with his nephew continued to mount. Beethoven had not inherited a robust constitution. No matter how virile his music may sound– indeed, it is hard to find its like – Beethoven suffered from all sorts of illnesses throughout his life. Ignaz Xaver Ritter von Seyfried, his friend from roughly 1803–4, wrote in a biographical appendix to his book of 1832 on Beethoven's studies in figured bass that the composer "had never known ill health." This was far from true. As a child Beethoven, like Mozart, had contracted smallpox, disfiguring his complexion. At the age of 16 he apparently suffered from serious asthma attacks, perhaps as a psychosomatic reaction to the death of his mother. Reporting the death of his mother to Joseph Wilhelm von Schaden in a letter of 15 September 1787 (see page 20), he wrote: "Since my return [to Bonn] I have enjoyed very few happy hours. For the whole time I have been plagued with shortness of breath, and I even fear that it may develop into consumption. Moreover, it has been compounded with melancholia, a torment nearly as great to me as the illness itself."

From 1801 or thereabouts his letters and other documents abound in references to bodily complaints, usually abdominal colic. Writing in autumn 1805 to the singer Friedrich Sebastian Mayer while preparing the première of "Leonore," he exclaimed that "I cannot come, for since yesterday I have been suffering from colic pains, my usual ailment." Several attacks of influenza also appear in the sources, usually described as "rheumatic" or "intermittent fever" or "inflammatory catarrh." The most serious of these attacks began in October 1816 and lasted until summer 1817. After three relatively healthy years Beethoven again fell ill in late autumn of 1820, this time for several weeks. More serious still was his attack of jaundice in 1821, which may have permanently weakened his constitution: "Please don't think me a rogue or an absent-minded genius," he wrote to Franz Brentano on 12 November 1821, – "Since last year and until now I have been constantly ill.

Moreover, during the whole summer I was suffering from jaundice, a complaint which lasted until the end of August. On orders from Staudenheimer [his physician] I had to move to Baden in September. As the weather soon turned cold in that part of the country, I acquired such a violent case of the runs that I had to stop the cure and rush back [to Vienna]. I am feeling better now, thank God, and my return to health has at last begun to revive my spirits so that I can again devote my life to my art, as has not been the case for the last two years."

Only three years remained to Beethoven from the première of the Ninth until his death. These years were not happy ones. With regard to his art, they were dominated by the exhausting labors on his final great compositional testament, the "late string quartets." In his private life, they were tainted by his conflicts with his nephew Karl.

Karl was now eighteen years old. Until 1823 he had lived entirely at boarding schools, apart from a brief interruption in 1818. Time and again his mother, Johanna van Beethoven, tried to contact him, and above all to contest the custody settlement of 1816. The custody court had pronounced its final decision in 1820. Not only did Karl's mother lose the parental custody of her own son, she was forbidden to enter into relations with him without Beethoven's consent. Three years later Karl earned his leaving certificate from the boarding school headed by Joseph Urban Blöchlinger. He moved into his uncle's quarters and embarked on a study of classical philology at Vienna University. His first-year final examinations were scheduled for June 1824; Karl, however, proved to be unprepared. The same pattern was repeated in February 1825. By then Beethoven, having broken with his private secretary and subsequent biographer Anton Schindler, had begun to entrust many private errands to his nephew. In the early part of May 1825 Karl switched to the Polytechnic Institute to complete a commercial degree. From then on he no longer lived with his uncle, but was a boarder at the home of Mathias Schlemmer. Again he took on many secretarial duties for his uncle, who tried to monitor his every move. In 1826 this even led the composer to forego his annual summer holiday in the country. Karl was left with no freedom of action. Finally, disaster struck. On 6 August 1826, high in the ruins of Rauhenstein Castle in Helenental near Vienna (see plate 51 on page 91), he tried to put a bullet through his brains. Seriously wounded, he asked to be taken to his mother. Beethoven, too, must have been informed immediately, for he quickly dashed off a note to his physician, Dr. Karl von Smetana (letter no. 2181): "A great misfortune has happened, a misfor-

Plate 51
Helenental near Vienna. Oil painting by Norbert Bittner
Niederösterreichisches Landesmuseum St. Pölten

Plate 52
Karl van Beethoven (1806–1858) in cadet uniform
Photograph after an anonymous miniature, 1827
Beethoven House, Bonn

tune which Karl has accidentally brought upon himself. There is, I hope, still time to save him, especially by you if you will come soon. Karl has a bullet in his head: how this came about you will find out in due course. But come quickly, for God's sake come quickly."

The wound proved to be relatively harmless. Beethoven transferred the guardianship of Karl to his boyhood friend Stephan von Breuning (see pages 21 and 50), who finally granted the young man's longstanding wish to become a soldier. On 2 January 1827 Karl travelled to Iglau to enter the Eighth Moravian Infantry Regiment. A picture of him in cadet uniform appears on page 92 (plate 52). On the next day Beethoven drew up his first will. In it, he declared that Karl would inherit his entire estate. Three days before his death he added a codicil expressly restating his wish to make Karl his sole heir.

It is against this gloomy backdrop that Beethoven produced five of his greatest masterpieces: the "late string quartets." His contemporaries could only guess at their significance, and they have remained a source of inspiration to the present day.

As early as 18 May 1822 the publisher C.F. Peters in Leipzig had asked Beethoven for some new compositions (letter no. 1465). In particular he specified "symphonies for orchestra, quartets and trios with pianoforte, [and] solo items for pianoforte … Granted, the artist's muse will not be bullied, and anything you wish to send me will be welcome, for I am seeking contact with you not from self-interest but from a sense of honor." Beethoven responded on 5 June by offering Peters the "Missa solemnis," the "Diabelli Variations," and several other works both new and old, including "a quartet for two violins, viola, and violoncello, which I can also deliver at short notice for fifty ducats." It is highly unlikely, however, that he had done any preliminary work on the quartet. This was probably one of those not infrequent cases when Beethoven was simply misleading a publisher with disinformation.

Nonetheless, it may well have been Peters's inquiry that prompted Beethoven to return to this genre after such a long hiatus. For in fact, as the "Missa solemnis" and the Ninth Symphony amply demonstrate, his mind was set on large-scale forms. Writing to Peters on 20 December, he confessed that "if my income were not entirely <u>without substance,</u> I would compose nothing but operas, symphonies, church music, at most [!] some quartets." (letter no. 1516) It is thus only fitting that his two unfinished works from this period are another symphony and a grand overture on the name of BACH.

In any event, the ground had been prepared by Peters's suggestion. Then, on 9 November 1822, Prince Nikolaus von Galitzin (see plate 53 on page 95) asked Beethoven whether he "could be imposed upon to compose one, two, or three new quartets, in which case it would be my pleasure to pay him whatever amount he might think appropriate." (letter no. 1508) Beethoven expressed his willingness on 25 January 1823, and even went so far as to announce the completion of the first quartet by the end of February or, at the latest, by mid-March. Evidently he set to work immediately, for there are extant quartet sketches dating from February 1823. They bear no resemblance to op. 127 in its final form, however, and the other sketches for this quartet all originated in 1824–5, thereby postdating the completion of the "Missa solemnis" and the Ninth Symphony.

Eventually Prince Galitzin's "one, two, or three quartets" became a total of five. Apart from op. 127, all of them were published posthumously: opp. 127 and 131 by Schott in Mainz, opp. 132 and 135 by M. Schlesinger and A.M. Schlesinger in, respectively, Paris and Berlin. Opus 130 and its original finale, the "Grosse Fuge" ("Great Fuge"), were issued by the Viennese publisher M. Artaria (see plate 54 on page 96). In other words, some of the opus numbers were not assigned by Beethoven. Nor do they reflect the order in which the works were composed: opp. 127, 132, 130, 131, and 135.

The first of the late quartets, op. 127, was premièred by Beethoven's old comrade-in-arms Schuppanzigh on 6 March 1825. The performance was ill-starred. There was not enough time to rehearse. Beethoven, who was present at the rehearsals, felt called upon to upbraid the four musicians (letter no. 1940):

> Most excellent fellows!
>
> Each of you is receiving herewith his part, and hereby pledges himself, on his word of honor, to be irreproachable in his behavior, to acquit himself with distinction, and to vie in excellence with the others.
>
> Each of you who is participating in the said undertaking must sign this sheet of paper.

> Schuppanzigh mp   Beethoven
> Weiss
> Lincke mp the great master's accursed cello
> Holz
> the last of all, but only in point of his signature.

Plate 53
Nikolaus Borisovich, Prince Galitzin (1794–1866)
Photograph after a lost miniature
Beethoven House, Bonn

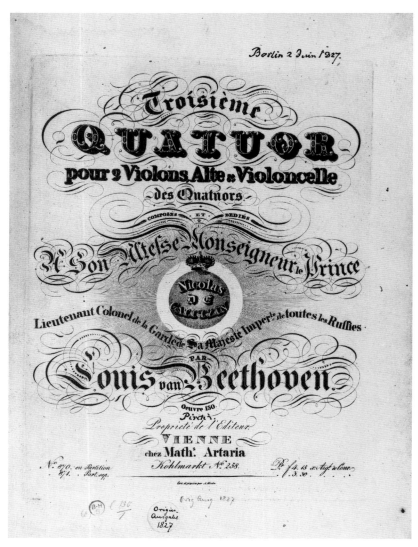

Plates 54
Ludwig van Beethoven, String Quartet in B-flat major, op. 130
Title page of first edition
Beethoven House, Bonn

Plate 55
Adolph Martin Schlesinger (1769–1838)
Photograph after an unsigned oil portrait
Beethoven House, Bonn

Despite these precautions, the performance was a failure. Beethoven, fully aware of the work's innovative qualities and obviously concerned about gaining the audience's approval, pressed for a second performance with another leader. The performance duly took place on 23 March, with Schuppanzigh's place now taken by Joseph Böhm. It was reviewed in the Viennese THEATERZEITUNG on 28 April 1825: "The result of that performance [with Schuppanzigh] was a frank admission on the part of almost everyone present, professors no less than amateurs, that they had fathomed little or nothing at all of the goings-on in Beethoven's tone poem ... Now a staunch art-lover and connoisseur has put on a new production of the quartet ... with Professor Böhm taking the part of the first violin ... The good professor played this marvellous piece twice on the same evening ... in such a way that nothing else was left to be desired ... and the noble creation glowed in all its brilliant glory."

Other reviews were less favorable. Beethoven hastily sought to placate Prince Galitzin. In a letter drafted on 13 July and sent to Karl for copying, he jumped to his work's defense (letter no. 2006): "Don't pay any attention to the drivel in the newspapers . . . The quartet failed in its first performance with Schuppanzigh, it is true, but only because he needed more time than ever before due to his corpulence ... Since then it has been played six times to perfection by other musicians, and always to rousing applause."

All the same, Beethoven's contemporaries found the late quartets difficult to comprehend. Ludwig Rellstab, a leading critic of the day, concluded a review of opp. 127, 130, and 132 for the BERLINER ALLGEMEINE MUSIKALISCHE ZEITUNG with the following words: "Those who realize that even the mightiest genius is, and must be, subject to finite laws will have to concede that even in a Beethoven the auditory memory must become weaker, and the living colors of the tones must gradually fade. Perhaps many things in his divine imagination sound different to our mundane and sluggish ear; and without wishing to presume, we would like to retire in humility and merely remark, that any genius who has suffered such an intrinsic alteration to and disturbance in his faculties, must needs produce and create in a different manner from one who stands and moves about, powerful and intact, in the living world of the senses. It is therefore not our place precipitously to attack those things that seem to us strange and incomprehensible, but merely to acknowledge that where there is no common sense of proportion, there can be no proper appreciation. Let no one, however, conclude from the above that Beethoven's most recent work is therefore incommensurate with our understanding. No, thanks be to heaven, there are still sufficient bonds between him and us to ensure a common language for our feelings, even if this language is not always intelligible in its nethermost and subtlest ramifications ... O, thou mighty genius, who hast granted us such bounty from thy divine inspiration, shouldst thou alone be made to suffer? No, eternal nourishment and exaltation doth spring from such a fount, and thou shalt keep and comfort and exalt thyself although not a ray of the dulcet tones thou hast miraculously created shalt e'er penetrate the mute and soundless night of thy earthly existence."

Two things become clear from these lines. First, the listener's inability to understand this music – or to understand it completely – is blamed on the deafness of its creator. Second, the composer's deafness and sufferings are marshaled to help erect that Beethoven myth that would dominate virtually the entire nineteenth century and is still in evidence today. Of course contemporary audiences had difficulties with these quartets and their new and strange idiom; many listeners still do so today. But they obviously recognized the value and beauty of this music, its significance and profundity. They *liked* it. Why else would Beethoven's brother Johann have written in a conversation book, following the première of op. 130 on 21 March 1826, "the entire town is talking about your latest quartet; everyone is delighted at it."

Beethoven must have lived in constant fear of material want at this time of his life. One reason was surely his failing health; another must have been his self-imposed obligation to care for his nephew's present and future needs. He refused to touch the bank shares he had purchased years before, although they were now worth several thousand gulden. Instead, he complained time and again at great length about his straitened circumstances. This may explain why he sold his second quartet to Maurice Schlesinger, despite his bad experiences with him in the publication of the last three piano sonatas (see plate 55 on page 97). Schlesinger was probably the first publisher to offer Beethoven more money for a quartet, and he promptly received the contract. In early September 1825 the publisher paid a visit to Vienna and wrote the following note in Conversation Book no. 94: "As I already told you, I will not negotiate with you, but will settle on a price beforehand." A few pages earlier we read: "If you write quartets and quintets you will earn more money for your nephew than from all your other big works put together. You should therefore work on these quartets on the side. He who lives with the wolves must learn to howl with them, and nowadays, as we all know, the world is a wolf's den."

Schlesinger had found Beethoven's soft spot. The two men quickly reached an agreement, and Beethoven took great pleasure in Schlesinger's visit as a welcome diversion and enrichment. It was at Schlesinger's request that the A-minor String Quartet, op. 132, was performed privately to a select audience at the "Wild Man" inn on 9 September 1825. The performers were the Schuppanzigh Quartet, Schuppanzigh having been restored to grace. Their conversations at the inn are recorded virtually complete in the conversation book reproduced on page 79.

Schlesinger's contract with Beethoven specifically mentioned two string quartets. By the time he left Vienna, however, he could only take along the engraver's copy of the A-minor Quartet; the second, in B-flat major (op. 130), was still incomplete. For various reasons Beethoven was persuaded by his closest confidant of these years, Karl Holz, to sell the work to Artaria. Thanks to Holz's intervention, Artaria visited Beethoven for the first time in mid-January 1826. The contract for op. 130 had already been signed on 9 January, and Artaria expressed his thanks in his first entry in the conversation book: "I am extremely pleased that you have placed your trust in me and allow me to publish a beautiful work from your pen! You will have every reason to be satisfied. The entire piece will be fully engraved by a week from today."

As it happened, the engraving was not finished until August. Artaria then caused his intermediary Holz no small amount of embarrassment in another matter. According to Holz's own account, he was given "the extremely delicate task of persuading Beethoven to write, in lieu of the nearly unintelligible fugue, another finale more amenable to the comprehension of the public ... Beethoven asked for time to think it over, but on the next day I received a letter in which he expressed his willingness to grant the request."

The fugue, as we all know, was indeed extracted and published separately as op. 133, with Beethoven's own arrangement for piano four-hands appearing as op. 134. Both editions of the "Great Fugue" bore a dedication to Archduke Rudolph, Beethoven's longstanding friend and patron, who had received many dedications from Beethoven in the past.

The next quartet, op. 131, was originally meant to bear a dedication to Beethoven's old friend Johann Nepomuk Wolfmayer. At the last minute, however, the composer changed his mind. On 10 March 1827, two weeks before his death, he relayed his wishes to his publisher Schott: "According to my letter the quartet was to be dedicated to someone whose surname I have already sent you. But something has happened which has decided me to alter my request. The quartet must now be dedicated to Lieutenant Field-Marshal Baron von Stutterheim, to whom I am indebted for many kindnesses." Stutterheim was head of the regiment which Beethoven's nephew had joined in early January following his failed suicide attempt. It was he who had arranged for the young man's appointment as a regimental cadet. In the end, however, Wolfmayer received a quartet of his own. One of the last conversation books informs us that Beethoven pronounced the dedication of his final quartet, op. 135, on his deathbed. "Dolezalek paid a visit to [Wolfmayer] yesterday," wrote Holz around the middle of March. "He said the dedication would be the happiest moment of his life."

Keeping yet another promise, Beethoven then sold this final quartet to Schlesinger, thereby honoring his contract of September 1825. On 30 October 1826, while visiting his brother's country estate in Gneixendorf, he sent Schlesinger an engraver's copy for the edition in parts. The cover letter reads as follows (letter no. 2224): "Just see what an unfortunate fellow I am! First of all, it has been difficult to compose this because I was thinking of something much greater. I wrote it solely because I had promised it to you and needed the money. As you will gather from the *'es muss sein'* ['it has to be,' the motto of the fourth movement; see plate 56 on page 103], the work did not exactly flow from my pen. As if that weren't enough, I wanted to send it in parts to make it easier to engrave, and I couldn't find a copyist in the whole of Mödling. So I had to copy it myself. Well, wasn't that a bit of drudgery! Ugh, it is finished. Amen."

Beethoven had to interrupt his work on the five quartets several times due to illness. Evidence of this can be found in his original heading to the third movement of the Quartet in A minor. The autograph reads: "Heiliger Dankgesang eines Genesenen an die Gottheit in der lidischen Tonart" ("a holy song of thanksgiving from a convalescent to the Divinity, in the Lydian mode"). All that remains of this subtitle in the print are the Italian words "Canzona di ringraziamento" ("hymn of thanks"). Along with the commotion surrounding his nephew's attempted suicide, this illness ensured that by the midsummer of 1826 Beethoven was urgently in need of a holiday. Karl had been ordered by the police to leave Vienna, a suicide attempt being regarded in those days as a criminal act. Finally, Beethoven accepted an invitation to visit his brother Johann, with whom however he was on the worst of terms for many reasons. A portrait of his brother can be found on page 104 (plate 57).

Little is known about Beethoven's stay in Gneixendorf. Several accounts maintain that he was poorly housed and fed there and even had to pay for his stay. None of these claims is verified by his brother's and his nephew's many entries in the conversation books. It is quite true, however, that the brothers quarreled violently, and that Beethoven left Gneixendorf precipitously at the end of November. At his arrival in Gneixendorf he had already revealed symptoms of a liver ailment known as "dropsy." Now the illness broke out in full force on his return trip to Vienna. The drafty coach only added a case of pneumonia to his ills. But it was probably the liver disease that caused his death.

Back in Vienna, Beethoven was confined to bed; indeed, he was hardly able to stand up. In the four months remaining to him he tried, with remarkable composure, to settle his affairs. He wrote letters to friends and publishers; he read the proofs of several quartets and drew up his will; he even began to compose a string quintet, as Schlesinger had suggested (see page 99). In short, he by no means fell apart. He was surrounded by many of his friends: Zmeskall, the companion of his early Vienna years, inquired after his health; Baron Gleichenstein, J.N. Hummel, and Schuppanzigh came to visit; the Streicher family of piano makers saw to his wants, as did his boyhood friend from Bonn, Stephan von Breuning. Breuning's thirteen-year-old son Gerhard visited the ailing man, a welcome distraction. Holz and Schindler, now reinstated in Beethoven's good graces, resumed their secretarial services now that his nephew had joined his regiment in Iglau.

Beethoven died on 26 March 1827 in his lodgings in the so-called "Black Spaniards' House" (named after the Spanish Benedictine friars), where he had been living since October 1825. There are several conflicting accounts of his final days. The account below was presented by Schindler in a letter of 12 April to the publisher Schott:

> When I came to him on the morning of the 24th of March I found his entire face distorted and so weak that he could only communicate with the greatest effort, speaking two or three words at a time. Shortly thereafter the university professor [Wawruch] arrived, who said to me, after a moment's observation, that he was proceeding with rapid steps to his appointed end ... Beethoven then said to me: "One last request: please write to Schott and send him the document [the declaration of ownership of

Plate 56
Ludwig van Beethoven, String Quartet in F major, op. 135
Autograph of first violin part
Beethoven House, Bonn, H.C. Bodmer Collection

Plate 57
Nikolaus Johann van Beethoven (1776–1848)
Oil portrait by Leopold Gross
Vienna Historical Museum

op. 131]. He will need it. And write him in my name, for I am too weak. I kindly ask him to send the wine he promised. Write to England as well if you can find the time.

The pastor came around midday, and the function proceeded with supreme edification. Only now did he seem to believe that his end had come, for hardly had the clergyman left the room than he told me and the young Herr von Breuning: *"Plaudite amici, comoedia finita est!* Didn't I always say it would end like this!"

The Latin quotation translates as "Applaud, friends, the comedy is over!" and was used to end comic plays in the days of ancient Rome. In 1874 that same "young Herr von Breuning" published a slender volume of memoirs in which he claimed to recall "with absolute certainty" that Beethoven quoted these words not after receiving extreme unction, but one day earlier after a final conference with his physicians. Schindler continues:

At this moment a clerk from Privy Councillor von Breuning's office entered the room bearing the crates of wine and the punch you had sent. This happened at about quarter to one in the afternoon. I placed the two bottles of Rüdesheimer wine and the other two with the punch on the table near his bed. He looked at them and said: "Pity, pity, too late!" These were the last words he ever spoke. Shortly thereafter he fell into such agony that he could no longer utter a sound. Toward the evening he lost consciousness and fell into a delirium. This lasted until the evening of the 25th, when visible signs of death became apparent, but only ended at quarter of six on the evening of the 26th.

The painter Josef Danhauser took Beethoven's death mask on 27 March. It can be seen on page 107 (plate 58) and presents a somewhat distorted replica of his features. Before the mask was taken, some bones had been removed near Beethoven's ear during an autopsy in the hope of establishing the cause of his deafness. Nonetheless, the death mask remains a moving and immediate testimony to the great composer.

The funeral took place on 29 March 1827, three days after Beethoven's death. At first his body was laid out in state in his lodgings. Then the coffin was carried to the Church of the Holy Trinity in Alserstrasse. Thousands of mourners followed the coffin (see plate 59 on page 108); many sources speak of 10,000 people, and some even of 20,000. Among them were his brother Johann and family, and apparently his sister-in-law Johanna van Beethoven, the mother of his nephew Karl, who remained with his regiment in Iglau. Also present were many representatives of the Viennese aristocracy, all of his surviving friends, and many fellow musicians: composers, singers, violinists, pianists, publishers, and many more, including Franz Schubert and Carl Czerny. After the consecration in the church, the procession walked to Währing Cemetery, where the actor Heinrich Anschütz declaimed a funeral oration written by Franz Grillparzer.

Währing Cemetery was closed in 1873 and transformed into the so-called "Schubert Park" in 1925, Schubert having been buried there a year and a half after Beethoven. In 1888 his remains were removed to the so-called "Grove of Honor" in Vienna's Central Cemetery. This tombstone is pictured on page 109 (plate 60).

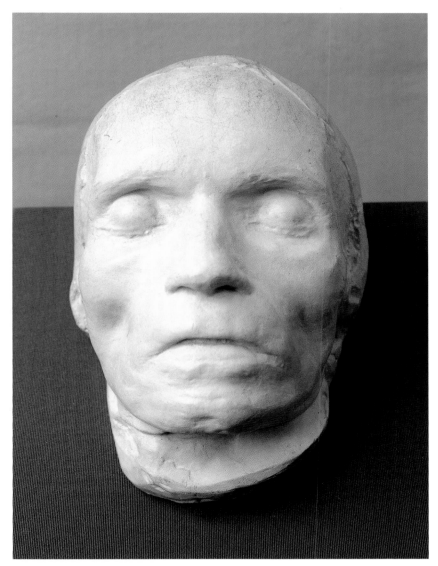

Plate 58
Ludwig van Beethoven. Death mask by Joseph Danhauser
Beethoven House, Bonn

Plate 59
Beethoven's funeral procession
Watercolor by Franz Stöber, 1827
Beethoven House, Bonn

Plate 60
Beethoven's tombstone by August Stauda in Vienna's Central Cemetery
Photograph from c. 1895/1900
Beethoven House, Bonn

BIBLIOGRAPHY

Readers may be interested in forming an acquaintance with other writings on Beethoven beyond this brief illustrated biography. The list below is meant to serve as an introductory guide.

The Letters of Beethoven, ed. and trans. Emily Anderson, 3 vols. (London: Macmillan, 1961).
   The standard English translation of Beethoven's correspondence. The complete German edition is *Ludwig van Beethoven: Briefwechsel Gesamtausgabe*, ed. Sieghard Branden-burg, 7 vols. (Munich: G. Henle, 1996–7).

Ludwig van Beethovens Konversationshefte, ed. Karl-Heinz Köhler, Grita Herre, and Dagmar Beck, vols. 1–9 (Leipzig: Deutscher Verlag für Musik, 1968–88) and vol. 10 (Wiesbaden: Breitkopf & Härtel, 1993).
   A complete edition and transcription of Beethoven's "conversation books." A helpful index in English was published by Donald MacArdle: *An Index to Beethoven's Conversation Books* (Detroit: Information Service, 1962).

Georg Kinsky: *Das Werk Beethovens: Thematisch-bibliographisches Verzeichnis seiner sämt-lichen vollendeten Kompositionen*, ed. Hans Halm (Munich: G. Henle, 1955).
   The complete and indispensable thematic catalogue of Beethoven's works, in German.

Donald W. MacArdle: *Beethoven Abstracts* (Detroit: Information Coordinators, 1973).
   An exhaustive resumé of all writings on Beethoven to date.

O. G. Sonneck: *Beethoven: Impressions of Contemporaries* (New York: G. Schirmer, 1926; repr. New York: Dover, 1967).

Beethoven Remembered: the Biographical Notes of Franz Wegeler and Ferdinand Ries (Arlington, VA: Great Ocean Publishers, 1987).
   A translation of the first Beethoven biography by two of his closest friends.

Anton Schindler: *Beethoven as I Knew Him,* ed. Donald W. MacArdle (Chapel Hill, NC: University of North Carolina Press, 1966).
    A translation of Schindler's biography in its third edition of 1860.

Alexander Wheelock Thayer: *Thayer's Life of Beethoven,* ed. Elliot Forbes, 2nd edn. (Princeton, NJ: Princeton University Press, 1967).
    A conflation of the many editions of this seminal nineteenth-century biography.

Maynard Solomon: *Beethoven,* 2nd revised edn. (New York: Schirmer, 1998).
    A sensitive biography with a penetrating view of Beethoven's psychology.

Maynard Solomon: *Beethoven Essays* (Cambridge, Mass.: Harvard University Press, 1988).
    A continuation of the preceding, with an annotated edition and full translation of Beethoven's diary.

Joseph Kerman and Alan Tyson: *The New Grove Beethoven* (New York: W. W. Norton, 1983).
    A useful short critical biography by two outstanding authorities.

Carl Dahlhaus: *Ludwig van Beethoven:* Approaches to his Music, trans. Mary Whittal (New York: Oxford University Press, 1987).
    A magisterial study by the leading German scholar of his day.

Scott Burnham: *Beethoven Hero* (Princeton, NJ: Princeton University Press, 1995).
    A modern look at the Beethoven myth.

Joseph Kerman: *The Beethoven Quartets* (New York: W. W. Norton, 1966).
    The definitive study of a genre that spanned Beethoven's entire career.

Donald Francis Tovey: *Beethoven,* ed. Hubert J. Foss (Oxford: Oxford University Press, 1965).
    A readable and provocative account of Beethoven's musical style.

1	2	3
G	G	X

Đổi	không đổi
G = 33%	G = 66%
X = 66%	X = 33%